OUR MIRACLE CALLED LOUISE

OUR MIRACLE CALLED LOUISE

A PARENTS' STORY
by Lesley & John Brown
with Sue Freeman

**PADDINGTON
PRESS LTD**

NEW YORK & LONDON

Library of Congress Cataloging in Publication Data
Brown, Lesley, 1947—
  Our miracle called louise.

  I. Fertilization in vitro, human.   2. Sterility,
Female—biography.   3. Brown, Lesley, 1947—
4. Brown, Louise, 1978—   5. Infants—England—
Biography.   I. Brown, John 1941— joint author.
II. Freeman, Sue, joint author.   III. Title.
RG135.B76   618.1   79–15292

ISBN 0 448 22073 3   (U.S. and Canada only)
ISBN 0 7092 0051 X

Filmset in England by SX Composing Ltd.,
  Rayleigh, Essex
Printed and bound in the United States
Designed by Colin Lewis

In the United States
PADDINGTON PRESS
Distributed by
GROSSET & DUNLAP

In the United Kingdom
PADDINGTON PRESS

In Canada
Distributed by
RANDOM HOUSE OF CANADA LTD.

In Southern Africa
Distributed by
ERNEST STANTON (PUBLISHERS) (PTY.) LTD.

In Australia and New Zealand
Distributed by
A.H. & A.W. REED

*John and Lesley Brown dedicate
this book to :*

*Mr. Patrick Steptoe and Dr. Robert Edwards,
who made Louise's birth possible ;*

*Mrs. Sheena Steptoe and Miss Jean Purdy,
who have been such kind friends ;*

*and to the memory of Lesley's Gran,
Mrs. Hilda Rowsell.*

CONTENTS

PROLOGUE

I NEVER GAVE UP hope of having a baby of my own, even though it was to take fourteen years.

When a doctor told me, years ago, that it was a one-in-a-million chance that I'd ever have a child, I still kept trying.

Crazy as it sounds, even when Mr. Steptoe, the gynaecologist, warned me that a baby had never been successfully conceived outside the womb, I still wouldn't believe him.

It was my last chance. It had to work for me.

"Think pregnant," Mr. Steptoe now tells women like me, who would go through anything to have a child.

That's how I thought. And the result was our miracle called Louise.

LESLEY BROWN

CHAPTER ONE

Lesley didn't have a father. He walked out when she was two.

MOTHER WASN'T AROUND much either when I was a child. She always seemed to be going out somewhere, in her heavy, big-shouldered coat and a hat with a feather in it. But that didn't bother me until I was ten years old, when I was sent away to a children's home.

Mother, or Mum, as we called her, was about to marry her second husband, a bloke called Roy, and there was no room at his mother's house, where they were going to live, for my younger brother David and me.

We couldn't stay at my grandmother's house either. That was where we had lived for as long as I could remember. In fact, it was Gran who had brought us up while Mum was out at work.

It hadn't occurred to me that David and I were getting too much for Gran. In her long, flowery dresses and flat, lace-up shoes, she had always seemed old to us, but when we got up to mischief, she still managed to chase us up the stairs.

Grampy, as my grandfather was called, sat beside

the backroom fire when he came home from work, in a thick, old-fashioned suit with turn-ups and a high-buttoned shirt. He told us jokes as he smoked his way through packets of Capstan full-strength cigarettes.

There was so much for Gran to do that she never seemed to sit in her chair on the other side of the fire. She had her grown-up son, Peter, who was mentally retarded, to wash, dress and care for as well, so I suppose she couldn't have coped with us once Mum had gone.

One day Mum showed David and me a leaflet with a picture of a white farmhouse with lambs playing in the fields outside. The sky was bright blue. It had never looked that colour above the roof of Gran's old terraced house in Bristol.

The farm was in Australia, and there was a plan to send children there to help on the land, though we would still have to go to school.

Mum asked me if I would like to live in Australia. The farthest I had been from Gran's house was on a day trip to the sea at Weymouth, so I hadn't much idea where Australia was. I looked at the leaflet with the blue sky again and said that I would.

There was a big, dark staircase which wound down to a basement at the children's home where we were sent before going to Australia, and all the children walked down it in a line from the dormitories each morning to clean our lace-up shoes.

The home was also an assessment centre. A coach had taken us to a big house, buried in the countryside somewhere in Kent, to see if David and I were suitable for our new Australian home.

"Come out, Lesley. I know you're in there." A harsh voice beat against the door of a toilet at the home. I had bolted myself inside.

When I got up to mischief at Gran's, I always made

for the bedroom in which David and I slept and rushed into the furthest corner of a big oak wardrobe, where I would hug myself tightly. Gran, panting from the effort of chasing me upstairs, would grope furiously among the line of clothes.

"Come out. I know you're in there."

There was no wardrobe like Gran's in the children's home, so I had locked myself in the toilet instead. Nothing of me could be seen under the door, as my legs were curled up on the toilet seat.

Mine were fat legs, probably because I was such a terror for sweets. A boy had noticed them in the shorts we had to wear to play in the field beside the home.

"Hey fatty," he yelled. "No wonder your mum didn't want a fatty like you."

I had hit him hard before I ran away. Now, perhaps if I stayed quiet for long enough in the toilet, the harsh voice would give up and go away, as Gran always did. I don't remember her ever catching me when I hid.

Footsteps echoed down the long, empty corridor, past dormitories with lines of white-covered beds. There was a line of little hooks outside the toilets as well, where we hung our face cloths and towels. Every cloth and towel had a child's name on it. My name was now on everything I owned.

"She's in there alright," the same harsh voice whispered to another outside the toilet door.

Someone spoke in a gentler tone. "Lesley, your brother's crying. He thinks you've run away."

David often cried when we fished for tiddlers at a boating lake and I would hide from him behind the trees. I bullied him, and even hit him if he didn't do what I said, but I never let other children push David around. No one but me was allowed to upset my little brother. So I unbolted the toilet door.

A hand grabbed me. "Now, Lesley," said the second voice, which wasn't gentle any more, "You'll have to learn how troublemakers are treated here."

After that most of my time at the home was spent in bed. It was the punishment for everything, including bedwetting, and, big as I was, I had even started doing that.

But lying in the dormitory among the white-covered beds, while the other children yelled and ran about outside, still wasn't as bad as walking in a line to school each morning. The other children always seemed to snigger and whisper as we filed into the classroom and took our places at the wooden desks.

I kept to myself at playtime when David ran off with the other boys.

"Haven't you got a mother?" one girl asked me.

"Of course I have," I retorted. I never admitted that I was looked after by Gran. "My Mum's in hospital for a bit, that's all."

The girl rushed back to tell her friends, who stared curiously at me as she repeated what I had said. I turned my back on them and looked over the school wall at the street outside, which was like the one I used to play in when I lived at Gran's. But now I wasn't even allowed outside any more.

Those girls probably thought I was such a hard, tough kid. They didn't realise how much I hurt inside.

My bed in the dormitory was narrow, and not a bit like the big one with its curly iron headboard that David and I shared at Gran's. We jumped up and down on our bed so that it shook and rattled. One night we had jumped so hard that it had collapsed.

Gran still kept up the blackout curtains from the war, hoping the darkness would send us to sleep early, but it never did. We had a little yellow nightlight which made wax that we ate like chewing gum. When David started nodding off, I would carry the light into the big oak wardrobe, where I used to hide, to see my dolls.

They were so tiny. I made them beds out of match-boxes, and they slept in a line. I had promised them a pram as well, so I went on and on at Mum, which was my usual way of getting things, until she gave me the money to buy one. But I couldn't find a small enough pram anywhere, so I ended up with a colouring book from the corner shop instead.

As I lay in the dormitory, I wondered if it was Sunday at Gran's. It could have been. Since I had been in the home, I had lost track of time.

Gran would have baked a rice pudding in the scullery, while Grampy would still be sitting by the backroom fire, since we never went into the front room – not even on Sundays.

Gran kept her best furniture in there, such as a three-piece suite which, like everything in Gran's home, looked as old as she was. There was a bookcase full of books we never read, and a black metal statue of a boy dangling a little clock from his hand. I had never been inside the front room long enough to find out if the clock worked.

We had a proper, cooked breakfast of eggs and bacon on Sunday, and Grampy always left his bacon rind. David and I fought over who should have it, and we fought again over who scraped the rice pudding bowl at dinner time.

There was no bathroom in Gran's house, so each Sunday evening she put us in an enamel tub in front of the backroom fire. Grampy fiddled with the wireless, which was out of our reach on a high shelf of the dresser, with a budgerigar in a cage on the shelf above, and listened to a programme about the Ovaltine children while we had our bath. Mum sent for a song sheet with the tunes they sang, so we could join in.

"We are the Ovaltinies . . . happy girls and boys . . ."

The children at the home started to file into the dormitory. As they climbed into their beds, whispering to each other, I buried my head in my pillow, pretending to be asleep.

If I ran away, I would never find Gran again. I had no idea where Bristol was.

As the other children fell asleep, I started to cry. I was crying for my Gran.

As I grew older, and especially when I was told I could never have a child, I often wondered why Mum didn't seem to want David and me when we were young. She put us second to the new man in her life. But it must have been hard bringing up two children on her own.

She washed us in the enamel bowl on the backroom table every day before we went to school, and she always made sure we looked nice in matching jumpers and cardigans that she knitted herself. At night she often put us to bed with a bag of sweets to keep us quiet while she went out again. She often had to do extra work as a cinema usherette at night to earn the money for our keep.

No one ever mentioned father, since he had disappeared when Mum was expecting David. I didn't know much about this new man of hers either, as Roy hardly ever came round to Gran's.

Roy was a smart-looking bloke, quite tall, with a little moustache, and he had known Mum even before she met my father. They had got together again when father walked out.

It had seemed like a treat when Roy and Mum had taken us to Weymouth, since we rarely went on day trips to the sea. But children seemed to bore Roy, and he got fed up when David and I wanted to hang about building sand castles on the beach.

He didn't talk much, so I didn't bother to speak to him. By the next day, as I rushed out of Gran's house to play among the wrecks of old cars piled up on a dump near the bus depot and watch the green, double-deckers come and go, I had forgotten all about him. He was just a man that Mum knew. I never expected her to marry Roy.

That girl who had dared ask about my mother was still boasting when school finished. Arm in arm with her friend, she pushed past me, as the other children rushed out of the school gate to get home for tea.

Why was I different? Why didn't I have a mother waiting at home for me?

As it turned out, I wasn't suitable for Australia. A naughty child like me, who had hit a boy and wet her bed, certainly wasn't wanted there.

So Aunty Peggy, Mum's younger sister, rescued David and me. Although she already had two small children of her own, she took me to live with her. David was sent to a boarding school in Taunton and stayed with us during the holidays.

I didn't mind going to live with Aunty Peggy. Before she married, she had lived with us at Gran's. When she came home from work, she would often sit David and me on her bicycle and wheel us round the block. I had been a bridesmaid at her wedding, and David was the pageboy. When she and Uncle David lived in rented rooms near Gran's when they were first married, I would go round on Saturday afternoons and help her bake little cakes.

Now they lived in a modern, three-bedroomed house in Filton, a suburb of Bristol, which was a good bus ride from Gran's. That was to be my new home.

Aunty Peggy was glad that I hadn't been wanted in Australia. She had never wanted me to go all that way. And neither, as I later found out, had Gran.

CHAPTER TWO

*As teenaged Lesley struggles to grow
up, she meets John.*

THE CAFE WHERE I started spending most of my
time was called the Holborn. As it was close to
Bristol Docks, seamen of all shapes and colours,
with tattoo marks up their arms, and elsewhere if you
cared to look, came in. The cafe was a pick-up joint.

My mouse-coloured hair had been dyed platinum
blonde. Since I had just left school and earned my own
money in an underwear factory, machining corsets, roll-
ons and surgical hose, I had bought myself a two-piece
suit. It had a little jacket and a tight skirt in red with
green squares, so it looked like tartan. I fancied I looked
a lot smarter than my friend Carol, who always was a
bit of a mess.

Carol's nickname was Hopalong, since she walked
with a limp after having had polio as a child and she
would never wear a built-up shoe. That didn't make her
backward though, and she took me to pubs around the
docks, where I would have a shandy, which is a mild
drink, and a packet of crisps. Carol drank anything that
was offered, though it was usually beer, and always got
herself chatted up by Irishmen.

Aunty Peggy hadn't approved of Carol when we were at our secondary modern school, because she always reckoned I was easily led. But I felt old enough to do what I liked. That's why I had left Aunty's house and gone back to live with Gran.

Aunty was a good mother, but at that time she was a strict, churchgoing woman as well, and she didn't like my ways as I was growing up. She and Uncle David went to church twice a week and three times on Sundays, and Uncle played the accordion at the Sunday School service.

Now she and Uncle are divorced. Aunty no longer goes to church and even smokes cigarettes, though at that time she wouldn't allow any in the house. Sometimes I puffed one out of the bathroom window while I was having a strip wash. I was as much of a terror for smoking as I was for sweets. I spent all my school dinner money on packets of cigarettes.

Aunty Peggy caught me smoking once as I was walking down the road. She only went out once a week, other than to church, and that was on Tuesday, when she would go to have a chat with a friend for a couple of hours.

I had forgotten it was Tuesday as I tottered down the road in my stiletto heels which Mum had bought me. Stilettos were all the rage at that time, along with multi-coloured net petticoats and sloppy joe sweaters. I had gone on and on at Mum until she bought me a pair. It wasn't difficult getting what I wanted out of Mum in those days. Since she'd married Roy, she only came to see me on birthdays and other special days. So she usually bought me what I wanted to make up for it.

Mum always made sure I had a good time, too, when she took me out to restaurants and cinemas. But I always felt unsettled when she had gone again. Sometimes I wished that she never came to see me at all, though I was glad that I had those shoes.

Aunty said the shoes weren't suitable for a girl of my age, but I loved them all the same. I stitched them up with a needle and thread as they fell apart.

I was on my way to Carol's house to put on my makeup, which was something else Aunty didn't allow, when I lit a cigarette. I had been longing for one since tea.

I realised it was Tuesday when I saw Aunty leap off the bus. I threw the cigarette away, but it was too late.

"I saw you smoking!" Aunty cried. She marched me back home and into the living room, where she took the packet of cigarettes, broke each one in half, and threw them into the grate.

Uncle David was in the garden shed, where he spent most of his life, fiddling with bits of watches and clocks, as he was a watch repairer by trade. So I picked the halves of cigarettes out of the grate and smoked them when Aunty went out again.

"If you go on like this, you'll end up in another children's home," Aunty threatened when we had another row.

David and I had spent a few weeks in a children's home when Aunty had gone into hospital for an operation before her third child was born and there had been no one to look after us. The thought of being sent back to another of those places was more than I could stand.

I crept out of Aunty's house with my suitcase one evening while she was making tea. It was only a good bus ride home to Gran's.

Gran understood me. She never let me down.

"You can stay here child," Gran said. "I'll never let you go into another home as long as I live."

But Gran didn't approve of the cafe either. It was the start of the coffee bar craze, but, apart from the expresso machine and the juke box that played all night, mine was a real dive, with plastic-topped tables and dingy walls.

"You'll end up a slut, too, if you keep hanging round this place," a bloke called John told me, as some of the cafe girls left with the seamen to go on board the ships.

When I first met John, he really irritated me. The first few times he had come into the cafe, he didn't talk at all, but once he had got to know a few of us, he never stopped.

If he sat next to me, I pulled hairs out of his arms, which were rather hairy. That would shut him up.

He thought he knew the lot too. But he didn't, because I never went on board the ships. Some girls who hung around the cafe were already on the game, but mostly they were girls who were just out for a good time, and the seamen provided that. There were often parties, with lots of drink, on the ships.

But I wasn't easy with men, and those girls had to pay for their good time, unless the seamen got too drunk and sent them home in taxis instead.

Not many months had passed since necking had seemed daring enough to me. It had never occurred to me that there were unmarried girls who went to bed with men.

"Come on," said John. "I'll walk you home. It's time a little girl like you was tucked up in bed."

Carol was in a corner, being given free handouts of cigarettes from another Irishman. She found the Irish irresistible, though she never could explain why.

It was two miles home to Gran's and I didn't fancy the walk alone, even though I didn't fancy John.

"Why do you hang around a dive like that?" he asked, as we headed away from the docks, with the ships' lights twinkling on the girls with their sailors, having their good time.

It often wasn't much fun sitting for hours over a cup of stone cold coffee, but at least no one told me what I should be doing, except, of course, for this bloke John.

"Why do you?" I retorted.

"Because I've got nowhere else to go," he said.

I might have expected that I would get his life story on the way home.

John was twenty-one, though he seemed a good deal older than that to me, probably because he had already been married and had a couple of kids.

His wife's name was Margaret, and he'd met her in the cafe as well. "She wore a suit like yours," he told me. "She was a quiet little thing as well."

But that hadn't stopped her running off with another bloke the previous Christmas Eve, leaving John with a baby of five months and a toddler of nearly two. No wonder he was always on about those cafe girls.

He hadn't been able to manage to look after his children and work as well, so the baby, Beverley, had been adopted by some childless relations of his. The elder daughter, Sharon, was in a children's home.

"I hate her being in a place like that. She's become such a skinny little thing," he told me.

I glanced at John as we approached Gran's house. He had a cheerful face under a mop of baby curls. He wasn't such a bad bloke when you got to know him. Even his voice had grown quieter now.

"You get inside, young Les," he told me, as we stood in the back alleyway behind Gran's house. He didn't even try to make a pass. He was a different sort of bloke.

The worst thing that had happened since I left school was losing my first job when they reduced the work force. Working in an underwear factory hadn't been what I had really wanted to do. For years I had imagined myself a nursery nurse, which is what Aunty had been before she married. Since I loved looking after her three children and taking them down to the clinic to get their free cod liver oil and orange juice, it had seemed the right sort of job for me.

But it meant staying on at school to pass exams, and I hadn't felt like doing that, especially as exams were mostly double Dutch to me.

Looking back though, I really enjoyed that first job of mine. It wasn't just any factory job, because I had six weeks' training at college to learn how to machine the underclothes. Gran had really liked some chairback covers which I had once embroidered for her. And, when Mum had a baby (my stepsister Lorraine) while I was working at the factory, I used bits of trimmings that were left over from putting the fancy frills on bras to make her a little dress. I was always quite good with my hands.

But the newcomers at the factory had to go. After that I got a job in a cafe owned by the father of a school friend of mine. That didn't last long though.

My school friend's name was Stella, and she was a Greek-Cypriot girl whose father was even stricter than Aunty Peg. It was Stella who took me down to the beach with her boyfriend while we were still schoolgirls. He brought his friend along to neck with me. I didn't fancy mine much, but Stella was crazy about her bloke. Her father would have nearly killed her if he had found out, because she was only supposed to mix with Greek-Cypriot chaps.

Stella's father tried the heavy hand on me when I worked for him. He threw my portable radio into the rubbish bin because it was playing too loudly while I did the washing up.

I didn't have to put up with treatment like that. He wasn't my father, and that radio had cost me several weeks' wages. So I walked out on that job.

A few weeks later, hanging about the Holborn cafe again, Carol and I were picked up by a couple of Irish blokes, and mine, being rolling drunk, was getting fresh with me.

John walked in and, as he stood at the cafe door looking round to see who was there, I beckoned to him.

"Come on, laddie," John said in his friendly way, picking the Irishman up from the seat next to mine. John was always a very strong chap.

"That's my bit of skirt you've got your hands on."

This Irishman was dying for a fight, so John and I left the cafe and he walked me back again to Gran's.

I had never really been out with John, but once or twice he had walked me home. One night when I'd had a few too many, he took me back on the bus. I really led him a dance too. I kept on trying to ring the bell.

"Got yourself a job yet?" John asked. That was always his first question when he came into the cafe each night.

By that time I wasn't working at all. There had been a job in a laundry, but the women there had been much older than me and they had bossed me around. So I started taking time off, and soon it was easier not to go in at all.

Gran hadn't realised yet. I left the house at the normal time every morning and just went down to the cafe instead.

"I'll have to tell Gran tomorrow that I've no money for my keep," I told John. "There will be a terrible row when she finds out."

Gran didn't seem much different from Aunty at that time. She didn't allow me to smoke in the house, and she was often waiting up when I got home late. It made me feel guilty when I saw the worry on her old, tired face.

"You must pull yourself together," John said. "I went off the rails a bit when Margaret left me, drinking and behaving daft, but I always made sure I had a job to keep me steady."

John still lectured me, but now I didn't mind so much. We talked about everything on those walks home.

Gran's house was in darkness, but she often nodded off as she waited for me by the light of the backroom fire.

John and I stood in the alleyway behind the house. He was such a sturdy, solid bloke and I didn't want him to go.

"Will you hang on for a bit to see if everything's alright?" I asked him, "If there's another row, Gran might even throw me out tonight."

John lit a cigarette as I unlocked the back door. Gran had been cooking cabbage. The smell still hung about the scullery.

Grampy's armchair stood by the embers of the fire. But Grampy was dead now. Nothing was the same as when I was a child.

The old staircase groaned as I crept upstairs and listened outside Gran's bedroom door. Her breath sounded like a sigh as she slept.

If I wasn't there, she would always go to bed early, and, at her age, Gran needed her sleep. She would worry about me if I went, but it wouldn't be the same as having me around to worry about all the time.

My suitcase was on top of the big oak wardrobe where I used to hide. I took a few clothes. I didn't have many, as I never had the money to buy much.

If I ran away, Gran wouldn't know that I hadn't got

a job, and I felt much better not having to face her with that.

Now I was more worried that John wouldn't be waiting when I got outside.

I scribbled Gran a note. "I'm going away to lead my own life, so you don't have to worry about me."

I didn't say where I was going or for how long. I had no idea what would happen to me.

When Gran got up, she always made herself a cup of tea, so I left the note propped up by the teapot.

John stared as I ran towards him with my suitcase.

"I'm coming with you," I said.

CHAPTER THREE

John is landed with Lesley.

I HAD NEVER HAD much experience of women, as my mother died when I was ten, which left Dad to bring up my elder brother, Keith, and me. We became a family of men.

Mum was perfection to me. I would have done anything for her, and I never went out when she was about the house. But if Keith wanted anything, he always went to Dad.

It was the same after she died. If Keith wanted a bike, he got one, whereas I had to do a paper round to save up for mine. He was bought records and I bought my own. I used to think our Keith could get away with murder as far as Dad was concerned. Yet, in my own way, I was close to Dad.

We lived in a prefab estate in a district of Bristol called Knowle West, which was on the edge of the country, and our garden led into fields. The prefabs had been built by the Americans after the war for families like us who had been bombed out of their homes. Ours, in St. Dunstan's Road, was bombed by the Jerries in '41.

When we moved into the prefab, the Americans were still building some of the rest with a work force of German prisoners-of-war, and Keith and I cadged chewing gum off the GIs.

Prefabs were a cheap type of housing, but they were wonderful homes anyway, kept warm in winter and cool in summer by thick, cardboard walls. And there was a real bond between the people on the estate, because we had all lived through the bombing in the war.

When Mum was ill, there was nothing our neighbours wouldn't do to help. The house was kept clean and there was always supper on the table. But when she died, Dad didn't seem to want help from anyone, probably because he didn't want to be seen in such a state.

On Saturday nights he brought home a weekly treat of pork bones and, as it got late, he warmed them up in the oven for us to eat. Keith had usually gone out, as he wasn't as shy as I was about mixing with people, so Dad and I sat in the firelight, chewing the bones and not saying much. We were never ones for a lot of chatter.

Dad had let himself go since Mum had gone. He had worked for years in the local iron foundry, driving a crane, and, every night without fail, when he came home he had a good wash and changed his clothes. But he didn't bother now.

It was the same with the garden. He had won prizes for that garden of his. There was nothing he couldn't grow in it, and we ate homegrown vegetables every day, while Mum made pots of gooseberry and blackcurrant jam. Now it had become as untidy as he was.

Big as I was, I curled up on Dad's lap on those Saturday evenings by the fire. While he dozed, I often thought about Mum.

She had been a semiprofessional actress when Dad met her. She was appearing in the chorus line of "Jack and the Beanstalk" at the Bristol Hippodrome at Christmas, and Dad was working the flies, which is what they call the curtains in the theatre.

It was a rebound romance for Dad. He had just been engaged to another girl. But a bloke in the navy had come home on leave and impressed this bird of Dad's with his sailor's uniform. Still, I don't think Dad worried about that once he had set eyes on Mum. As a child, I never heard them row or even swear at each other.

Dad sent me away when she was about to die. I thought I was the cat's whiskers going to stay with his step-sister Joyce in Bedminster, on the other side of Bristol, because Keith wasn't coming and we never normally went on holiday, except on a day trip to Bude with the scout troop each summer.

Of course I knew Mum was ill. She had been in hospital many times in the past three years and, when she came out that last time, Dad moved her bed into the front room. He had been told she had cancer.

On Sunday afternoons, Keith and I were thrown out, because mediums arrived to help Mum. This was Dad's way of trying to save her.

Once I had glimpsed the pain in her face. "What are you staring at?" she demanded, and I turned away. Mum couldn't die because I needed her.

The night she died, I hadn't been able to get to sleep at Joyce's house. The bedclothes seemed to suffocate me. I tossed and turned, and finally took off my pyjamas, which I often did at home. It always made Mum angry.

"You've only just put those on," she'd say.

I was still restless, so I crept down the stairs in my underpants to get a glass of water. Joyce and her sister Betty, who was staying, must have popped out, for Joyce's father was alone in the front room. He didn't notice as I slipped past the half open door to the kitchen. As I was running the tap, Joyce and Betty came in again.

Joyce's words made me stop dead on my way back upstairs.

"She's gone now," she said. Then she turned and saw me.

"Go straight back to bed," she told me. But her voice wasn't angry.

I lay in bed, thinking about the tea set I had saved my pocket money to buy for Mum. It was a beautiful set, as delicate as she was, and I had told the shop to hang on to it until I got home. I was so proud telling everyone that I was going on a holiday.

Now I would never go back to collect it. Joyce hadn't had to say any more. Perhaps it was because I was so close to Mum that I knew she was dead.

I was still crying when Betty, who was sharing my bedroom, came upstairs.

"I've got a tummy ache," I told her.

"It will be gone in the morning," she said.

Keith was only a year older than me, but he went to Mum's funeral. Dad didn't want me there. When it was over, Joyce took me home on the bus.

As we got off at the stop near the prefabs, she said: "John, your mum's gone."

"I know," I said.

"Who told you?" Betty looked shocked.

"No one. I just knew."

Betty put her arms around me, but I didn't cry. I had accepted that I wasn't going to see Mum again.

That same night I lay in bed with the door half open. It was a trick of Keith's and mine, so we could hear the wireless from the front room. But it wasn't switched on that night.

Mum's bed had gone, and the front room echoed

horribly as Dad moved around in there.

Perhaps I was dreaming, as Dad said I must have been, but, as I lay there, my mother seemed to stand in the doorway, looking down at me in bed.

She was as tall and slim as ever, with her delicate complexion and fine, black hair, flicked up at the ends as it had always been.

The fire had burnt down, as I sat remembering on Dad's lap.

Dad woke up with the weight of me. He pushed me off and stirred the fire. "Off to bed," he said.

There was never any argument about it. Dad was a small man with small hands and feet, like mine, and he only ever really hit me once, but I still respected him.

I was reading by torchlight under the bedcovers as he came up to bed. "I told you to go straight to sleep," he said, with a wallop over my head.

It was through Dad that I started going to the Holborn cafe. As I got older, I seemed to get on his nerves, since I hung around the prefab quite a lot. I was the type who was slow in coming forward, and I could never start a conversation even if I was in a crowded pub.

"Why don't you get out and enjoy yourself?" Dad often moaned. Eight years had passed since Mum's death, and Dad had smartened himself up again.

He was even courting a widow called Mrs. Dumphy who lived down the road. Her husband had died of cancer, just like Mum.

"Go down to the shop and buy a pair of nylon stockings. Never mind who for," he often told me.

But I knew who Dad gave them to, and I was glad he was getting about with Mrs. Dumphy now.

I was eighteen, and had already got through a lot of jobs since I left school. At that time, I was collecting rubbish for Bristol Corporation and had money to spend.

It was still quite a step for me though, to go to the centre of Bristol, because, since we lived on the outskirts of the city, I was really a country boy.

That cafe was a pick-up joint, and though I kidded myself that I only went there for a cup of tea, I was looking for someone too, though not among those girls who hung about the ships. I've never gone for women with a lot of makeup plastered over their faces. That's why Margaret struck me when she walked into the cafe.

She had on a smart costume, rather like the one Mum used to wear, and only a little lipstick and rouge on her cheeks. So we got together. But I don't expect I would have really settled down with Margaret if our daughter, Sharon, hadn't been born.

It was Margaret who asked me to marry her. It happened one afternoon when I went to the dentist and Margaret walked there with me, pushing Sharon in her pram. She was just four months old at the time.

On the way, we stopped off at a cafe and Dad walked in. He had never met Margaret, and knew nothing about Sharon. I had left home six months before and hadn't even been back for my clothes.

After going on at me to go out, Dad had started moaning about it once I did. He threatened to lock me out if I kept coming home late and, one night, after I missed the last bus again, he had kept his word.

"Sod you," I yelled, as I rattled the bolted door. I turned on my heels and walked away from the prefab back to Margaret's room.

"Dad, this is Margaret. And this is my daughter, Sharon," I told him when we met in the cafe. It must have been a shock for him, but Dad took it well and I left him talking to Margaret while I went to have my teeth filled.

"Why don't we get married," she asked afterwards, as we walked back to our flat.

It hadn't really crossed my mind before. We had a two-roomed flat and our own kitchen. We seemed fine as we were.

Margaret had settled me down. I still changed jobs every five minutes, but I didn't hang around that cafe any more.

I suppose that I loved Margaret in my own way, but I hadn't much experience of that. I had only been out with three girls before I met her and I had never got any of them into bed.

But now there was also Sharon to think about.

Two days later we married at a register office with Dad's step-sister Joyce and her husband as witnesses. Then Margaret started spending money I never knew she had.

"It was a wedding present from your Dad," she explained. He had given her £100 to marry me.

Dad could be generous, especially when he had a win on the horses, which he backed a lot. I remember the time a girl I was keen on spotted a costume in a shop window which cost £15. I just hadn't got the money to buy it for her myself.

When I asked Dad for a loan, he replied: "Sod off. I haven't got that sort of money either."

The next morning I found fifteen pound notes tucked under the sandwiches that I took to work.

Dad was also a man who faced up to his responsibilities. Now that he knew about Sharon, giving Margaret that money to get us married was his way of making me face up to mine.

Margaret left me three times during the year or so that we were married, and the last time was on Christmas Eve. I had a job mending cables for the G.P.O., which was clean work and quite well paid, so I had saved £130.

"Here you are missus," I told her, handing over the lot. "The turkey's ordered, so's the leg of pork. Buy some presents for the kids as well."

We had two by then. Beverley was five months old.

That evening, after a few drinks on the way home, I got in to find there was no food cooking on the stove.

"Hey, missus, where's my dinner?" I yelled round the kitchen door.

Our next-door neighbour was sitting in the other room. "Your wife left in a taxi soon after you went to work," she said. "She hasn't been back since."

The first time Margaret had disappeared, it didn't occur to me that she had gone off with another man.

She had been nineteen when I met her, the same age as me, and, although she had been to bed with other men, she didn't have a clue about sex. Not that I knew much about it either. My experience amounted to a bit of necking and groping with some girls in the alleyways behind the prefabs after dark. But, although I was keen on it, Margaret couldn't seem to care less about making love.

The first time she left me was while I was having my tea. "Mind the children for me. I'm just popping out for an hour," she said.

I didn't take much notice since she got depressed when she stayed indoors. As it happened though, that hour turned into four days.

Margaret had lost all interest in the flat since I married her. Usually I got down to cleaning up the mess when I got in from work. It didn't bother me, as I had to do that at home after Mum died. I always kept the prefab clean, so Dad wouldn't be ashamed to bring anyone back, just as Mum would have done. And that's how I tried to keep our flat.

39

What upset me more was the state Margaret kept the children in. Even other people commented about their scruffy hair and clothes.

That fourth day I caught up with Margaret as I pushed Sharon and Beverley in the pram past the statue of Neptune that looks out to Bristol docks.

In those four days I had become so frantic I had even reported her missing to the police.

Now she was being almost carried by two of the cafe girls as she crossed the street.

"Leave her alone," said one, as I started hollering at my wife.

"Can't you see she's been beaten up."

Margaret had been on board the ships. I took her home and cleaned up the mess a drunken sailor had made.

So that Christmas Eve, when she went missing again, I called the hospital, but I didn't really expect to find her there. A friend of hers called Thelma, who lived nearby, would know what man Margaret was with this time.

"Well, I suppose someone's got to tell you," Thelma said. "She's run off with a hotel porter."

Margaret had had a hard life as a child. She had run away from her home in Shepton Mallet because her father was a violent man who had often beaten her.

The bloke she left me for worked in a hotel in the Channel Islands during the summer, and he had promised to take her back with him. It must have sounded a glamorous life, better than the one I had to offer, with two kids and a two-roomed flat.

Thelma had the kids over for Christmas dinner, and I found a bottle of Scotch in a hamper the owner of a local liquor store had packed for me when I told him my wife had scarpered with all my money. I only had £3 left.

I drank my way through the bottle, and vowed that was my lot with women.

And now there was this girl Les.

I had fancied Les when I first saw her in the cafe. She had bright, blonde hair and a tartan mini-skirt. A real darling she looked.

"What a cracker," I said to my friend Frank.

"Keep your hands off. That's my tart," he replied.

When Frank got into some trouble and was sent away to Borstal, he asked me to keep an eye on Les.

"I've been asked to look after you," I told her.

Les glared at me. "I can look after myself," she replied.

She tried to appear tough, like the other cafe girls, but I saw through that. I guessed she was shy, because that's how I was myself. When I walked her home once or twice to her Gran's, I felt sorry for her more than anything else.

She was in trouble with her Gran and out of work as well. Sooner or later she'd be on the ships with the other girls. To my mind, Les was going downhill fast.

"Hang on a minute," she told me one night when I walked her home. And before I knew where I was, she was back with a suitcase in her hand.

"I'm coming with you," she said.

For a moment, I couldn't think what to do. Then I took her case.

"Alright," I replied, "I'll buy you a plate of chips."

CHAPTER FOUR

Lesley, John and Sharon become a family.

I WASN'T IN LOVE with John when I ran away from Gran's, but I thought a lot of him.

"You could have done better for yourself," said a woman who worked behind the counter at the Holborn cafe when she heard I had gone off with him.

There were men at that cafe who tried to get girls on the game. John always said I might have gone that way too if I hadn't taken up with him. To my mind, he was the best of that lot.

There had been a bloke called Frank, who was coloured and a bit of a layabout. But Frank wasn't as bad as the rest so, when we went to his room above a junk shop, I let him make love to me. It was my first time, and a big step from those necking sessions on the beach when we were terrified of going the whole way. Most girls didn't in those days.

But the cafe girls did, and they talked so much about it that I wanted to find out for myself what they were on about. It wasn't that Frank meant much to me. Making love was like going to the cafe. It made me feel grown up.

42

But, as I've said, John was a different sort of bloke. He didn't try anything on the first two nights we spent together, and that made me think even more of him.

When we made love, it was in a shabby bedsitting room, with naked light bulbs and bare floorboards, but it had a double bed. It seemed so natural when it happened that we didn't even talk about it. But the next morning, as we walked down the street, John put his arm round me.

Apart from that, being away from Gran's wasn't as I had imagined it. The first night after I ran away, John and I slept in some disused railway carriages that stood in a siding in Bristol near where we live now. The carriages were known at the cafe as a last resort, and we had nowhere else to sleep.

After we had eaten our plate of chips, we waited at the cafe until it got too late for anyone to be about. Then John led me across a bridge through a field which glittered in the moonlight with a March frost. Another couple were already installed in the carriages, so we searched along the corridor for a compartment that was cleaner than the rest. John slung my suitcase in the luggage rack, pulled down the blinds, and we curled up on opposite sides of the compartment along the line of seats, without even taking our shoes off in case we had to make a run for it.

I was only sixteen, and too young to have left home without Gran's permission. If she woke in the night and found me gone, she might have already put the police on my track.

If I thought that Louise, when she reaches the same age, might run off and live like that, I would be worried stiff. Gran was as precious as a mother to me, but all that really mattered as I lay in that railway carriage was that there was no one to tell me not to smoke or what time to get in. It was only when I had a child of my own that I realised how Gran must have felt when she found I had gone.

The next morning the door of our compartment was thrown open, and a pale, drowsy face, that looked as if it hadn't been long out of bed, stared down at us. There was a black railway cap on the man's head.

"I beg your pardon," he said, as if we were being disturbed at the Ritz, and closed the carriage door.

"That's torn it," cried John, shooting up the blinds to watch the railway worker disappear over the frosty fields, scratching the back of his head.

"He's bound to tell someone. We can't stay here again."

We had a wash and another plate of chips at the cafe, and then John and I tramped the streets, looking for a room to let. But accommodation was scarce, and cheap rooms hard to find. Landladies looked suspiciously at the two-shilling ring from Woolworths that I had stuck on my wedding finger, and my one suitcase, and shook their heads.

We didn't last long in the rooms we did get. We left one in a hurry by the back door as a police car pulled up at the front. It seemed that Gran had almost caught up with us. We waited for hours at the cafe, until it got late enough to sneak back and collect our things.

As it turned out, we needn't have bothered, because we lost everything, apart from the clothes we stood up in, the following week. A Pakistani landlord, who thought we were going to leave without paying the rent, seized the lot, and we weren't in any position to report him to the police.

The worse it got, the more people seemed to take advantage of us. There was a Puerto Rican called Cornelius who played a nasty trick on us. He often hung about the cafe, boasting about the property he owned and flashing a thick wad of notes. There were some tall stories told in the cafe, and his sounded taller than the rest. Although Cornelius was a lot older than us, he looked a proper layabout. Where he got all that money was a mystery though, since he never seemed to work.

But when Cornelius told us there was a room for us in his own house, I wanted to believe him. The night before, John and I had spent at a courting couples' haunt called Brandon Hill, huddled together on the grass under a chilly ceiling of stars. We hadn't had much sleep, because we kept hiding behind a bush each time a policeman did his rounds. If we didn't find a place today, it would mean another night under those stars.

"You'll have to see my missus about the room," Cornelius said. This sounded strange as he always made out it was his house.

"Don't tell her you're not married either. She doesn't approve of people who live in sin."

The front door of an old, four-storey house was opened by a huge woman with a tiny head. No wonder Cornelius always seemed terrified of his wife.

Her name was Kate and she was a domestic science teacher. She sounded as if she was still making herself heard at the back of the class.

John was blushing, but I was speechless, so he managed to explain that we had come about the room. "You'd better see my husband," boomed Kate. Cornelius was huddled in front of a television set. He was a scrawny little chap.

Cornelius had told us not to let his wife find out that he already knew us, so he pretended to take no notice as she showed us around the house.

"Money won't be a problem," John assured her. He had a steady job at the docks.

Kate's house was untidy, but that room was like none we had seen since I had left Gran's home. It even had a carpet and light shades. It was just what we needed to better ourselves. We could settle down and lead a decent life.

"You two are married, I suppose?" Kate demanded.

Nervously, I twisted my pretend wedding ring. John was blushing again. "Of course," he replied, but the way he said it, it didn't sound like the truth. Cornelius was still staring at the television set.

Kate began to look uncomfortable too. She shot a glance at her husband's back. "You've got your marriage licence on you, I presume?" she asked.

All that mattered now was to get out of that house. Quick as a flash, John replied: "We'll bring it round when we collect our things."

But we hadn't got any things either, since we had left the Pakistani's house.

Cornelius began to rock with laughter as he sat in front of the television set.

"See you later," said John, as we left, with Cornelius' laughter still ringing in our ears. The last person I thought that we could ever face again was Kate.

But although we never went back for that room, we became friends with her later on. It was Kate, as it turned out, who had all the money and gave Cornelius his wad of notes. She even owned their house.

She couldn't have cared less that we weren't married. It was Cornelius who had set us up. He had told his wife to ask to see our marriage licence, so he could make fools of us. Cornelius often beat his wife, and she was so terrified of him that she always did what he asked.

But all we knew that night as we left their house was that it was probably Brandon Hill again for us.

Sharon, John's elder daughter who was in the

children's home, was often on his mind. He kept on about finding a decent place so we could have her to live with us. Those scruffy bedsitting rooms with their bare floorboards and naked light bulbs were no place to bring up a child. But after months of drifting from one to the next, our luck changed.

Our new West Indian landlady was even more devout than Aunt Peggy had been. There were religious pictures hanging all over her house, which was also nice and clean, and she went to the Pentecostal Church each evening where she prayed for her husband, who was always going gambling instead of going to work.

John and I had two rooms and a shared kitchen, so it was almost like a proper flat and, since I helped the landlady to look after her two children while she went to work, it would have been easy for me to have Sharon as well. I wanted that.

The home where Sharon was reminded me of the ones that I had been in as a child. The children there had tiny sandwiches, not much bigger than postage stamps, and a bowl of dolly mixtures for tea. No wonder Sharon's arms and legs were like matchsticks. She could have been a Biafran child.

John often bought her new clothes, and so did his Dad, but, as always happened in those places, they had disappeared. She wore someone else's tight-fitting, brown cardigan and corduroy trousers that hung down because they were too big. I had had to wear odd bits of clothes like that in the homes I had been put in. When I had told one matron what size bra I took, she replied: "You take what fits. We don't go in for sizes here."

Sharon stared at me, as John tried to explain who I was, but it was difficult for a three-year-old to understand.

"Mummy," she cried, as she ran to me. She couldn't

47

remember what her real mother looked like. She had mistaken me for her.

Since John didn't live with his wife, he wasn't allowed to have Sharon. So we worked out a plan to get her back. He told me what to say and I wrote it down, because his spelling never was that good.

My hand was trembling when I dialled the number of the children's home. "I'm a welfare officer from East Ham," I said in my best voice when the matron answered the phone.

John had picked East Ham because it was the only place far enough from Bristol that he knew, as he had worked there for British Rail for a while.

"I've just seen Sharon Brown's father," I continued, down the phone. "He's got a nice flat here and he's back with his wife. So I'm recommending that Sharon lives with them."

It was only three years since I had been a child in one of those homes. The matron there always looked at me as if I was dirty too, after she had gone through my satchel and found a dirty joke.

"When will Mr. Brown be collecting his daughter?" asked the voice on the phone. I couldn't believe that anyone like that could be polite.

"He'll be there in an hour and a half," I replied, and banged down the receiver. There was no time to waste before that matron discovered her mistake.

"She's got no toys," cried John, as Sharon munched her way through a plateful of fat sandwiches at our flat. There were bottles of cod liver oil and jars of malt in the cupboard to build her up.

We had made so many plans for Sharon's homecoming, it seemed impossible that we had left something out. John rushed to the newsagent's across the road and returned with a little truck.

I had knitted a white cardigan with a pink edging for Sharon, so I took off the tight-fitting, brown one and put it on.

"Thank you, Mummy," she said. She's called me that ever since.

It had been six months since I had run away from home, and lately, especially when Sharon arrived, I often found myself thinking about Gran.

I couldn't have faced her when John and I were living such a rough, uncertain life. But now there would be no more shifting from one scruffy room to the next, no more late cafe nights and endless plates of chips. I wasn't ashamed of the way it was now, and I wanted to tell Gran how I had made out.

"So you've turned up again," said Gran, as John and I stood on her doorstep.

Her voice sounded as if she hadn't been worried, but her eyes told a different story. Gran looked John up and down.

"You'd better come in," she said.

John sat in Grampy's chair, while I perched on the arm and told Gran what I had been up to, or at least the bits she wouldn't mind.

The house looked as old as ever, and so did Gran. She didn't say much, but then she never did. She started on John though, when I went upstairs to fetch the rest of my things.

"Are you going to marry the girl?" she asked. I leant over the banisters to hear what he'd say to that.

"We've only just got ourselves settled. We've got to make sure it's going to work out," he told Gran.

John tried to hold my hand as we walked away from Gran's house.

"What's up with you?" he asked. I just shrugged.

What he told Gran had upset me, but I wasn't going to let on that it had. John guessed, though, that I had overheard.

"Look, Les, I'm playing fair with you. I don't want to get married again, after the mess I made of it with Margaret.

"It might have worked out with her if we hadn't married. We got along fine until we did.

"And now, we're happy as we are, aren't we?"

Not being married hadn't worried me at first. There had been so many other things to think about from day to day, and the future was where we would be sleeping the next night. But it was different now that we were settled with Sharon as well.

John and I hadn't planned how long we would stay together. It was just that, since I'd left Gran's, it had never once occurred to us to go our separate ways. At times it had seemed as if we only had each other, and we had got so close we went everywhere together. I just couldn't imagine being without John.

"Anyway, luv," he said, as we walked down the road. "How can I marry you? I'm not even divorced."

That was a good excuse. John said he didn't know where to find Margaret, as he hadn't heard a word since she'd walked out on him. But to my mind he hadn't even bothered to try.

Sharon was watching from the landlady's window. "Mummy . . . Daddy," she called when she spotted us.

John's face was always cheerful when he saw me with his child. He would have married me straight away if I got pregnant, because he was that sort of bloke.

But that hadn't happened, even though we never did anything to prevent it, and not getting pregnant had begun to worry me a bit.

Sometimes I wondered if it was because I felt guilty about not being married to John that stopped me from having his child.

John came into the kitchen as I got the tea. He never could stand it when I got into a quiet mood.

"I've thought of a way to make a fortune in our old age," he said. "We'll have enough kids to start our own first division football team."

I had always wanted a big family. Ten, I thought when I was a child. But when I got more practical, I would have settled for as many as we could have afforded to bring up. Three or four would have been about right.

At that moment though, just one baby of our own would have been enough.

I don't know what made me think the way I did when John talked about our football team. There was no reason to imagine that I wouldn't get pregnant. There were couples I knew who had tried for ages before they'd had a baby, and we hadn't been together all that long.

But as John went on talking, a voice inside me told me something else. At that moment I knew it wasn't going to be easy for me ever to have a child.

CHAPTER FIVE

When John strayed.

THIS WOMAN I met called Janet wasn't all that much to look at, though she was small and slim and didn't wear much makeup. She made a tremendous omelette as well.

You could say our affair started over those omelettes of hers. She cooked some when a mate of mine called Terry, who was knocking off her girlfriend Maureen, took me round to Janet's house.

Janet and Maureen were a couple of married women who liked a bit on the side, though they both had two young children. Maureen's youngest was just a baby, but that didn't stop her fooling around.

She and Terry kept kissing and giggling, and finally they disappeared into a bedroom, leaving me looking like an idiot with Janet.

"Come on," she said at last. "Help me do the dishes."

She started to talk about her husband, who worked on building sites and fancied himself as a ladies' man, though he wasn't much shakes in bed by the sound of it.

I don't quite know how it happened, but as soon as we sat down again we started to neck. Before I knew where I was, I found myself in Janet's bedroom.

Dad's words came back to me. "Once you've made a decision, stick to it, lad." Janet was in a high old state, but I struggled off the bed. If I didn't get home soon, Les would be wondering what had happened to me.

As far as sex went, I was still a learner. The first time, before I married Margaret, had been a disaster. Dad hadn't mentioned the subject, so I had listened to what other chaps said they got up to and looked at those glossy girlie magazines, and thought that I'd like to try some of that for myself.

It had never been that good with Margaret, but with Les it had been a different matter. I didn't try to make love to her right after she left her Gran's, because I was afraid of landing myself in more trouble. Les needed help, and I was only just getting over Margaret walking out. So for a while sex didn't come into it between us.

It happened at the right moment and, once it had, there was no one else on earth for me but Les. Wherever we went we had our arms around each other. But it wasn't just because of sex. In all ways, we couldn't have enough of being together.

Les and I had been with each other for about three years when I met Janet, and we still seemed a happy enough couple. But deep down was a different matter. If I had known why Les had gone off sex, perhaps I could have understood. But as it was we were too shy to talk about things like that with each other.

It had been a long time since I had felt wanted by a woman. But Janet was probably frustrated, whereas Les and I had a lot more going for us than just making love. By the time I reached home, I had decided there would be no more necking with Janet.

53

"What's that red mark on your neck?" demanded Les as I stripped off for bed.

It was a bloody big love bite. Les watched my reaction in the bedroom mirror.

"Oh, that," I said, as casually as possible. "I'd forgotten to tell you about that.

"Some blokes at work were mucking about and one put that on me so I'd have some explaining to do when I got home. And it looks as if I have."

Les didn't comment. It was often difficult to tell what she was really thinking. When something was up, she just went quiet.

She turned her back on me in bed, so I touched her gently.

"Lay off," she said. "I'm tired. Leave me alone."

I couldn't have touched her again for thousands of pounds.

Given the chance, I could fancy sex every night of the week and twice on Sundays. But not like that. It would have been more exciting to have gone round the corner with a prostitute for all the response I got lately from Les.

It had crossed my mind that perhaps it was because Les hadn't become pregnant that she had gone off sex. She had been to see a doctor who told her there was plenty of time, so I didn't expect her still to be worried about it. Les wanted a baby and, as far as I was concerned, that was fair enough. It would have pushed me into marrying her, but, after my mistake with Margaret, I wasn't in any hurry to do that. In the meantime though, having children wasn't the only reason for making love.

But the way Les carried on, it was as if there was a glass wall between us as we lay side by side in bed.

"Coming over to Janet's?" asked Terry one dinner break. Her house was near the factory where I worked, and I didn't need persuading to go. Since telling myself that I would never see Janet again, I had already been over to her house a couple of times in the past week. We still necked furiously, but we hadn't gone any further. Dad's words still held me back.

But when I popped over that dinner break, another voice inside me was telling a different story. "Why not have a bit of fun? You're not even married to Les."

Janet got all the feeling I had bottled up for months with Les.

Usually I felt clumsy in bed. Being my size, it was difficult to be gentle. But with Janet I didn't feel like a bull at a gate. By the end of another week I was obsessed with Janet. But I wouldn't have left Les if she hadn't told me to clear out.

It happened one night when Terry and Maureen ran off together. As Maureen had left her baby behind, I told Les I was going to search for them.

"Don't worry if I'm gone a while," I told her. It meant I could spend the whole night with Janet.

"Bugger off then," said Les. "Don't think that love bite fooled me. I know what's going on."

It was a relief more than anything. The strain of pretending nothing was up had been worse. I didn't want to leave Les, but I couldn't give Janet up. I wanted both of them.

"Janet's like an obsession," I told Les.

She had gone as white as a sheet. "I'll give it a fortnight," she said in a tight voice. "A month at the most. Then you'll get fed up with her, like you've got fed up with me."

I wasn't going to stand for that. "I won't ever need to look elsewhere," I replied. "Janet satisfies me, which is something you haven't done for a long time."

"Bugger off," Les screamed at the top of her voice.

55

In a daze, I moved towards Sharon's room.

"Don't you touch Sharon," yelled Les. "Her Mum's already left her. Now you're doing the same thing. But I'll never let her down."

I didn't even take any clothes. As I passed Les, I kissed her on the cheek. Janet was waiting outside.

It was just like the old days, as Janet and I tramped the streets searching for a room. The one we found looked just as scruffy as those Les and I had shared, and it even had a Pakistani landlord as well. There was a nymphomaniac on the first floor who entertained the postman, the milkman and all the meter readers when the man she lived with was at work.

The trouble between Janet and me was that we couldn't spend all the time in bed, and, when we weren't there, we had nothing to say to each other. It hadn't even taken a fortnight, as Les had predicted, for me to realise I had made a mistake.

Janet sat on the bed in a dressing gown, painting her nails, while I smoked another cigarette in the only armchair in the room. It occurred to me as I stubbed out my cigarette that I had just as little feeling for that ashtray as I now had for Janet.

What a bleeding idiot I had been. Les' potential as a wife had been staring me in the face, and I'd been too daft to take advantage of it. She had never complained about taking Sharon, even though I had made it clear I wouldn't marry her.

Janet was the one who was like Margaret. She had left her husband and kids to have a good time, just as Margaret had done to me. I wondered if that husband of Janet's had hit the whisky bottle, just as I had done.

It was six o'clock. Les would be putting Sharon to bed. She was just like a real mother to my child.

56

"Put that paint pot away," I told Janet. "We're going out."

Cornelius was at the cafe and, for once, I was glad to see him, because Les and Sharon had moved into his house. Les couldn't afford to keep our flat going without me there.

"Hey, I've some news," exclaimed Cornelius, his eyes twinkling. "Les thinks she's expecting."

Janet was at the counter, out of earshot, asking for a cup of coffee. I looked hard at Cornelius. You never could tell with that bloke whether he was telling the truth.

"Les says she'll never speak to you again," Cornelius continued. He was enjoying himself over this one alright.

"You'll have to think up an excuse if you want to see her," he said. "Ask for that sewing machine you bought Les for her birthday. You could always sell it. I expect you could do with a few pennies."

I've always thought a bloke of my size shouldn't be romantic. I bought Les chocolates and bunches of flowers, but I never told her that I loved her. I was too embarrassed to put feelings like that into words, and now, standing on Cornelius' doorstep, certainly wasn't the moment, especially since Janet had tagged along.

"What are you after?" Les demanded, glaring at Janet. "You're taking Sharon over my dead body."

"No, it's the sewing machine I've come for," I explained. "I'm a bit short at the moment, and it would fetch a few bob."

"Well, you're not having it," Les was shouting again. "You bought that machine for me."

It was Les' attitude that made me see red. I couldn't have cared less about that blasted machine.

"Well, I did pay for it," I replied, and then realised that I had said the wrong thing again.

"Clear off, the pair of you," Les replied.

"I hear you're supposed to be pregnant," I continued. It seemed quite a coincidence to have happened just when I had walked out. Perhaps it was a trick to get me back.

"That's none of your business any more," Les replied and slammed the door.

There was no point in going back to our room, so I took Janet to the Hartby Club, in the new Mecca Centre in Bristol, which I knew because I had worked there as a bouncer for a while.

Janet and I sat in our usual silence, while I knocked back a few pints. Her mood wasn't all that good either, after being confronted with Les.

"Do you want to go back to her?" she asked.

"Fat chance of that," I replied.

A sailor asked Janet to dance. It could have been one of those who had known Margaret as well, but I was past caring about that. It annoyed me though, the way Janet chatted to that bloke as they danced, when she never found much to say to me.

If she wanted to flirt, I wasn't going to sit back. I downed another pint and, without another glance at Janet, walked out of the club.

"Where's your sailor?" I asked.

It was about eleven o'clock when Janet returned. "You seemed to have so much to say to each other, I can't think why you haven't gone off with him."

She'd had a few gins and she was giggly, thinking I was jealous I suppose.

"He had to go back to his ship at Portsmouth," she said in a wobbly voice.

"Well, if you're staying here, I'm not," I replied. "Do what you want, but I've had enough. I'm moving out."

Janet's behaviour with that sailor had been the excuse I had been looking for. That was it, as far as I was concerned. But it took a while for Janet to realise I wasn't just jealous over her.

"I'll never look at another man again," she sobbed.

"I couldn't care less what you do," I replied. I was as callous as I thought she had been, walking out on her husband and two kids for a fling with me.

"Go back to your family," I told her as I left. "I'd give anything to be back with mine."

It must have been closing time at a pub called the Hen and Chicken as I walked past, after leaving Janet sobbing in the room. The late drinkers were falling out, and among them was Carol, or Hopalong as we used to call her when she hung around the cafe with Les.

Carol's taste for the Irish hadn't changed. She had a couple of drunken ones in tow. But she now had a reputation in Bristol of not being fussy about what man she went with. She had gone downhill in the way that I had once worried Les might.

"Hi, John," she said in a slurred voice. "I hear Les has shacked up with Cornelius. Remember that bloke, Frank, who she used to knock about with? He was coloured too, wasn't he? Les must have a soft spot for coons."

I grabbed Carol. "Don't you ever talk about Les to me like that," I said, shaking her. One of her Irish blokes made a grab for me.

"Look," I rounded on him. "You're too drunk to know what you're doing. I presume you're after getting her to bed, so take her there before she causes any more trouble."

He wouldn't do the sensible thing. When he took a swing at me, I drove a hard punch into him. He crumpled up in a ball. He was only a little bloke.

"Cor, aren't you strong," said Carol. "I don't know how Les could fancy that scrawny Cornelius after you."

I hit Carol with my knuckles. She took it on the chin and staggered back too senseless to say any more. The other Irishman had kept well out of trouble. He'd run away.

I had never hit a woman before, and I wasn't proud of myself. "I'm not with Les now," I told Carol. "But don't you ever say anything about her again in my hearing. You're not fit to mention her name."

Carol slid slowly down the pub wall to the pavement as I walked off.

I was ready to crawl on my hands and knees to get Les back.

CHAPTER SIX

How Lesley felt about John's affair.

WHEN JOHN LEFT, I put Sharon's coat on her and we just walked about the streets. Being where other people could see me made me pull myself together, and I might have done something stupid on my own in the flat.

The aspirin bottle only had four tablets left, but that was only a passing thought because I had Sharon to think about.

Men always let me down. The first one had been Father. He couldn't have wanted me either, or he wouldn't have walked out.

John had always seemed different. Other men chased after girls. Not him, I thought. But he had turned out exactly like the rest of them.

My cheek stung from the kiss he gave me when he left. I hadn't realised just how much I loved that bloke.

Sharon trotted beside me, holding my hand. It must have seemed fun to her, being out in the dark. She knew her father had gone, but it didn't seem to bother her as long as I was still there.

It had taken a little while to get used to Sharon's ways when she came out of the children's home. She was such a particular child. She wouldn't wear a dress with a speck of dirt on it. All her toys had to be put away in the right place each night, though you'd hardly believe it if you saw the state of her bedroom now.

Sharon knew I wasn't her real mother. We had made that clear before anyone else told her the truth. But it didn't make any difference. It was as if she was my own child.

"Where are we going, Mummy?" she asked. She was a strong child now, after I had built her up with all that cod liver oil and malt. But she was still very young and we must have walked a long way that night.

There was no one in my family to turn to. Aunt Peggy would think what had happened was only to be expected because John and I lived in sin. Gran might not have said it, but her look would have been enough.

"I could have told you so," would be what she'd think.

Then there was Mum, but she'd once been in the same boat herself.

"Let's go to Aunty Kate's," I told Sharon. Cornelius' wife had become a good friend.

Kate was up to her knees in washing from the launderette. There were always piles of washing around her house. Kate never seemed to iron a thing.

"There, there, my girl," she said, folding me in her great arms. Sharon was in the kitchen, amongst stacks of unwashed pots and pans, eating a bowl of stew. Kate's house may have looked a mess, but she was a tremendous cook.

"Good riddance, I say, if he's turned out like that," declared Kate in her massive voice which echoed around the house. At least Cornelius wasn't in to get some laughs out of this.

Those two were an ill-matched pair. Kate had long ago got herself into the family way with a probation officer, which wasn't done in circles like that. Her family were well-to-do in Preston where they lived.

It was then that Cornelius came along and, with an eye, no doubt, on the family purse, had married Kate and given her child his name.

But big as Kate was, she didn't dare stand up to Cornelius. He often hit their four children, but he was especially tough on Hughie, Kate's own boy, who was mentally retarded as well. He made the child wear boxing gloves to stop him biting his nails.

No wonder Kate thought I was well rid of John, after her experience of men.

"What's this woman of John's like?" asked Kate.

"Nothing special," I replied. "She's quite a bit older than me." I had only met Janet once. I didn't know why at the time, but I had taken an instant dislike to her.

John had had the nerve to take me over to her house. They had left me to look after Janet's two children while they went out to look at a washing machine that a friend of Janet's had for sale. Or so they said. John even told me he might buy it for me to save me doing so much work.

"Oh, the bastard," I cried to Kate. "I'll never speak to him again."

All the bits and pieces of suspicion had fallen into place. It had suddenly dawned on me when John said he would be out all night what was going on.

There had been something up with John, but I hadn't taken much notice of it. There are always ups and downs when you live with someone, and they usually iron themselves out. Even John's cock and bull story about that love bite on his neck had seemed almost true at the time, because I just didn't think he was that sort of bloke.

He still came home at the usual time, for he had sex with Janet in his dinner break, as I later found out. We had still been making love too, even though John said it was hardly ever. But I've never been one to want sex every five minutes.

"He even had the nerve to kiss me goodbye when he left with that woman," I told Kate.

Kate dropped a pile of washing and hugged me hard.

"I expect he'll turn up again like a bad penny," she said.

"Not until I say so, he won't," I replied.

Kate offered me the room in her house that John and I had once been so anxious to have. It suited her as well, because Cornelius always behaved himself better if there was someone else in the house.

It wasn't just because it was cheaper that I decided to take the room. It would also be harder for John to get Sharon if he had to get past Kate.

I knew from my own childhood what it felt like to lose a mother, and it wasn't going to happen to Sharon again. I would run away with her if it came to that.

Cornelius rushed in one evening after Sharon and I had settled into the top of Kate's house. His little eyes were blazing with excitement. He had been hanging around the cafe a lot.

"Hughie, where are your boxing gloves, you little bastard?" Cornelius yelled. Hughie cowered in front of the television set. The child wore glasses as thick as binoculars, but he still sat with his nose practically touching the screen.

For once Cornelius didn't thump him. He was too anxious to tell me the news.

"John's on his way round here with his woman," he cried, watching the expression on my face.

"What's he after?" I replied in a flat voice.

"He wants that sewing machine he gave you for your birthday. He's really hard up."

It sounded so unlike John. But then he wasn't the man I thought he was.

"He'll get a punch on the nose," I replied.

"Now don't get worked up in your condition," said Cornelius. "John knows you might be pregnant too."

Trust Cornelius to have told John that. I had suspected that I might be pregnant when John left, but there had been too many false alarms before to get worked up about that.

Almost every month I thought it must have happened, but it never had. John was probably right. Sex had begun to seem a waste of time when it didn't produce anything.

Now I almost felt pregnant. You can convince yourself of anything if you try hard enough, and perhaps that time I really was.

Somehow, too, I knew John would want to come back when he got tired of sex. What was more to the point, though, was how I would feel about him after he had put me through all this.

Kate found me crying when John and his woman had left. It was hard to accept that he had changed so much that he would ask for my sewing machine back.

By that time, however, I was in pain as well. If I was pregnant, it shouldn't have hurt so much. Something inside me must be dreadfully wrong.

"Have you thought that you might be pregnant?" the doctor asked after he had examined me. I hadn't mentioned that word to him. If the doctor said it, it must be true.

He handed me a letter to take to the hospital. "Gynaecological Department" was written on the envelope. "I must be pregnant," I told Kate when I rushed back. I was so excited I had forgotten about the pain.

When I told John that his affair would last a fortnight, or a month at most, I had secretly thought it might take a lot longer than that. So when he phoned to say it was all over with Janet, it was a surprise, since he had only been gone just over a week. It could have been a trick though, to get Sharon, so I left her with Kate when I went to meet him.

We had a cup of tea in a cafe, while John talked. I wanted to hear what he had to say for himself.

"I want you back, Les," he said after he had told me about getting fed up with Janet. He looked shamefaced.

"Well, you can't have me," I replied. "You're a different man now. After all you've put me through, how could you have asked for my birthday present back?"

"That was Cornelius' idea," John explained. "I wanted you, not that bloody machine."

But I wasn't going to rush back.

"At least let me see Sharon," he pleaded. "I promise I won't take her away from you."

She was his daughter. I had to trust him when he said that. He also asked if I was really pregnant.

"That makes no difference," I told him. "I can manage Sharon alone, so I can bring up another child."

It was my way of getting my own back. But I was almost sorry when John looked so upset.

"I've got to think this over," I told him. "I don't know what I feel any more."

"Fair enough," said John. "But won't you have

another cup of tea with me?"

Two weeks passed, and I was still thinking about going back to John, as I got ready for bed at the top of Kate's house. Sharon was already asleep in the other bed. It was a Sunday, and we had been out for a walk with John. He had kept his word about the child.

Suddenly, there was a noise on the stairs. Without even knocking, Cornelius burst into the room. He stood staring at me in my underclothes.

"Poor little Lesley," he leered. "All alone, without a man. I've come to put that right."

Cornelius had a reputation with the cafe girls. As he got closer, I smelt his breath. He was stinking drunk.

"Get out," I said. "Can't you see there's a child asleep in here."

Cornelius lurched closer. "Haven't I been good to you, Les? Given you a roof over your head? Now the time's come to pay me back."

I went to strike him, but he was better practised at that. He hit me so hard across the face that I staggered and almost fell across Sharon's bed.

Now Cornelius was enjoying himself. Lamps and tables crashed around us as he hit me over and over again.

Gradually, the effects of the drink slowed him down. He made a grab for me as I belted out of the door.

Kate stood on the landing below in her dressing gown. She had heard the noise and had guessed what had been happening in my room.

"Help me, Kate," I cried. "He's hitting me. I've got to get Sharon out of here before he starts on her."

Kate grabbed my arm. "Please stay," she pleaded. "He'll take it out on me and the kids once you've gone."

Kate might have been a good friend, but I had to put Sharon first. If Cornelius had laid a hand on her, I would have gone straight to the police.

Kate looked terrified as Cornelius appeared on the stairs. "Why are you sticking your nose into this, you great ugly bitch," he yelled.

Kate turned and fled into her bedroom, but Cornelius wouldn't let her alone. He was hitting her as I tore back upstairs.

Quickly, I dressed Sharon. She couldn't understand what was going on, she was so drowsy with sleep.

"We're going to find Daddy," I whispered, and, with Sharon in my arms, I crept down the stairs, past the awful noise that was still going on behind Kate's bedroom door.

John was staying about two miles away with a couple of married friends, Molly and Colin. Sharon and I walked all the way to their house, and that's how I went back to him. The right time had unexpectedly arrived.

They always say that it never rains unless it pours, and at that time, it was really like that. All I wanted was a bit of peace, when Janet turned up at our door.

It was only the day after I had run back to John. It looked as if our lives were going to be ruined again.

"Don't stand for it," said Molly, the woman whose house John and I were staying in. From the kitchen, I could see John talking to Janet at the front door.

I seldom lost my temper, but it was never forgotten when I did. I remember once turning on Aunt Peggy when she cut my hair.

She had been on at me for ages about it looking a mess, but I took no notice, as I quite liked it long. So she grabbed me and hacked it off. It looked like a crooked crew-cut from the front.

"You bloody cow," I screamed. Usually I was too afraid to swear at Aunt Peggy, but that time I made her sorry for what she had done.

Molly was still egging me on. "Go and find out what

that woman wants," she told me. "You're back with John now. Don't let her push you around."

At that moment, my temper snapped. I found myself standing beside John at the front door.

"If it's him you've come for, you're out of luck," I told Janet. I must have learnt a punch or two from Cornelius, for such a hard one landed on her nose that she fell backwards down the front stairs. She was picking herself up from the pavement as I slammed the door.

John just stared at me. He didn't say a word.

Now that we were back together, John and I had to look for another flat. It had to be big enough not only for Sharon, but for the baby I still thought I was expecting. But that didn't last for long.

The hospital doctor had written "ectopic pregnancy" on my card. I didn't know then that it meant a pregnancy in the Fallopian tubes. That he had written the word "pregnancy" seemed enough.

"There are complications," the doctor warned me. "You'll have to come back in a week, Mrs. Brown." I always pretended I was married at times like that.

I never went back. The pain inside me grew too bad to go to hospital. It would have meant doctors prodding and poking and sticking needles into me, and I preferred suffering on my own.

Whatever happened inside me sorted itself out, for when I woke up one morning the pain had gone.

If only it hadn't, for I knew for certain that morning that I still wasn't going to have a child.

"You're a lot keener on sex these days," commented John a few weeks later, after we had made love. "Having a bit of competition seems to have done you good."

But it wasn't only that. I had been so certain that I had been pregnant. If it had happened once, it could happen again. And I was trying hard.

CHAPTER SEVEN

John takes the plunge with Lesley.

Don't let Les fool you. She may appear a quiet little thing, but when she loses her temper I get out of the way fast, big as I am.

When she punched Janet on the nose, I was speechless, because I hadn't realised Les had it in her to do that. It was the first time I had seen Les in a rage.

It's been a good many years now since Les lost that temper of hers, but in those days before we married it flared up occasionally, for no particular reason, except perhaps because she still wasn't my wife.

There was the time when she forgot her keys. She banged on the window, while I made faces at her from inside the flat. Suddenly, her expression changed and, before I could duck, her fist came straight through the window and she landed one straight on my nose.

Her temper also ruined a brand new white shirt of mine. I had started driving lorries for British Rail by that time and, when I got home for my dinner break, I fancied a bit of a rest before I went back to do some overtime.

Les put a cup of coffee on the arm of my chair, but I nodded off.

"John, you've forgotten to drink your coffee." Les was shaking me.

"I'll drink it in a minute," I muttered, and fell straight back to sleep.

Les woke me by pouring the coffee down the front of my shirt. She happened to have a brand new blouse on that day, so I ripped it off her back. That will teach you, I thought, as I sat down again. Les rushed out of the room, and for a moment the house went very quiet.

But I might have guessed Les hadn't given up. Next she returned with a bucket of water and tipped it over my head.

She screamed with laughter at the sight of me, soaking wet. When she ran away, I chased after her into the kitchen, where she tripped and fell. For a second, I thought she had hurt her head, but as I bent over her, she was still laughing. So I threw a bowl of washing-up water over her.

That was enough for me, but not for Les. Screaming and shouting, she followed me into the front room. Because I took no notice of her, she got madder still.

The milk bottle which she threw next bounced off my chair, hit the ceiling, then the wall, and smashed into tiny pieces on the floor. Les was barefoot at the time, but she was too angry to think of that. She charged across the broken glass to land another punch on my nose.

It was always the same with Les. Once she thought that she'd beaten me, she calmed down. I bathed her feet, which were cut by the broken glass, cleared up the mess, and went back to work as if nothing had happened. And, in a way, nothing much had, because we were always closer after letting off a bit of steam.

At least we laughed together afterwards about blow-ups like that. It was more difficult to get close to Les when we talked over our worries late at night in bed.

Les often brought up the subject of Janet at those times, though it was months since I'd set eyes on her. The last time had been when Les sent her flying down the front steps.

"I still can't understand what you saw in her," said Les, as we lay side by side in the dark.

Why can't women understand the power of sex?

"If sex means so much to you, sooner or later you're bound to go off with someone else."

What I couldn't get into Les' head was that I would never risk losing her again. I worshipped the ground she walked on, but I was too embarrassed to tell her that.

"I love you, Les."

I turned my back on Les and buried my face in my pillow as I said those words.

Les switched on the bedroom lamp. "Did you say something?" she asked.

I couldn't repeat it when she looked at me. "Nothing important," I muttered, and she switched off the light again.

"If you go off again, I'll never take you back," she said. "Now, let's shut up and get some sleep."

Another of Les' late-night worries was about not having a child. It was beginning to bother me too, because the years were passing and it wasn't as if we weren't trying hard.

We still hadn't faced up to the fact that there was something really wrong, so we searched for excuses instead. Les had gone back to her old theory that she hadn't become pregnant because she felt guilty about not being married. There could have been some truth in that.

That relation of mine who had adopted my younger daughter, Beverley, had been trying for years to become pregnant, but it had never happened, even though doctors could find nothing wrong. Yet two months after she adopted Beverley she was expecting her own child.

There was nothing stopping Les and me getting married now, since I had finally got a divorce. Les worried that Margaret might turn up to get Sharon back. Even though that was most unlikely, because my wife had produced three more children by the man she'd gone off with, it was better to be sure that Sharon was completely ours.

Life for Les and me had become more settled than it had ever been. Bristol Council had turned a blind eye to us not being married and had given us a nice council flat.

A year had passed since I started working for the railways, and Les could hardly believe it, because I had never stuck to any job for so long.

Not that I was ever more than a day out of work, as I moved from one job to the next, but I soon got fed up with all of them.

It might have been different if I had lasted my apprenticeship at the iron foundry, which had been my first job when I left school. Most boys in those days followed in their fathers' footsteps, and it had been settled for ages that I would become a moulder at the same foundry where Dad had worked for donkey's years.

It was a respectable trade and, in my brand new overalls and thick boots with metal studs, I felt as proud as punch, though those boots made so much noise you'd have thought a carthorse was coming down the road.

My first wage packet was £2.3.7d., which to a lad of fifteen all that time ago seemed fine money. That first week, I handed over £2 to Dad for my keep, which left me only 3/7d. for the week, so Dad gave me a pound back.

It takes a lot to make me mad, but what I can't stand is being pushed around. The trouble at the foundry was that the foreman kept picking on me.

My first task was to make little round stop covers for water pipes and, because I wanted mine to look smart, I brushed them with graphite dust, to make them nice and smooth.

Graphite dust wasn't supposed to be used for that, and when the foreman saw what I had done, he walked through all my stop covers in his metal-studded boots.

Five days it had taken to make those nineteen moulds. As I sat among the broken pieces, I nearly wept.

Everything I did was wrong as far as the foreman was concerned, so one afternoon I walked out of the foundry in my overalls and boots and never went back.

I went through dozens of jobs after that. Welding pipelines, pulling pints, driving dustcarts, you name it and I've probably had a go at it. I've never been a milkman though. I never fancied that.

What I was after was a bit of freedom in a job, and I found that with British Rail, sitting behind the wheel of my eight-ton truck. My lorry took me to places I had never seen before, because we didn't have the money to go out of Bristol much. Driving along the open road, I felt like my own man, and that's what I've been doing ever since.

When I first started working for the railways, there was a painter called Nobby. I was his mate. I hadn't become a driver yet. Each day, when we were handed written instructions about jobs, Nobby always made out he couldn't read them because he had left his glasses at home. He always forgot those glasses of his, yet he never had any trouble when it came to seeing what was written on his wages' slip.

It didn't take me long to realise that Nobby couldn't read or write, because I had been in almost the same boat myself when I left school. Like Nobby, I never asked for help because, if you're illiterate, you don't want anyone to know.

Nobby got away with it too, being a crafty bloke. He had learnt to print his own name, and he never took an eyesight test, because he always made out that he'd left his reading glasses behind.

But I was a lot younger than Nobby and, when I left school, not being able to read more than a word or two in the newspaper worried me. I was bound to marry and have children of my own. What would they think as they grew up of a father who couldn't even help them with their homework?

At school it had been awkward enough. Not that I minded so much that my teacher knew, as there were a few other dunces like me. But being shown up in front of the whole class was a different matter. I always made an excuse to go to the toilet when it came to my turn to read out loud.

Shortly after I left school, by myself at home, I spread the letters of the alphabet on my bed and tried to fit them together. Then I got books out of the library and, with a dictionary, worked out what the words meant.

Reading went a lot faster than my writing, because I spelt words by their sound. For instance, for chemist, I wrote kemist, and, since I'm still no great shakes at spelling, I get Les to write my letters, though I tell her what to say.

By the time we moved to the council flat, there was a pile of books beside our bed because I was reading all the time. I helped Sharon with her homework too. When Les and I had kids of our own, I would have no problems keeping up with them.

There were no doubts left in my mind that I would be making another mistake by marrying Les. The only reason that I hadn't married her was that, after living together for six years, minus that week off with Janet, it was just a question of getting round to it. But anything was worth trying if it meant we could have a child.

I walked in from work one evening as Les was making tea and said: "Don't you think it's about time we got married?"

"Alright," she said. And that was it.

Les' hair was dyed black and, since it was permed as well, it went gingery in patches. To my mind, it looked a real sight, but I kept my mouth shut.

We all had new clothes for our wedding. Mine was a blue suit which went with Les' blue and white costume, and Sharon was dolled up in a pleated skirt and frilly blouse. Even her shoes were new ones, and Les curled her hair with hot tongs.

We told all the family that we were getting married. Dad himself had remarried by that time, but none of them, except for Les' brother David, turned up.

Kate, Cornelius' wife, who was the other witness, was waiting for us outside the register office in a huge stetson hat. Kate is one of those big women who like big hats, and that one looked really odd, perched on her tiny head.

Friday, August 23rd, was our wedding, and typical summer weather it was too. The wind was blowing up a gale when we stepped outside the register office after the ceremony. A photographer who hung around for couples like us who couldn't afford one of their own lined us up in a group for a wedding snap.

Kate hung onto her stetson for dear life, and Les' black hair stood on end as the wind howled round. Les kept giggling. She was in a state of nerves.

We couldn't afford a proper reception, so we went to a nearby cafe afterwards. There was some cream gateau on a plate, which would have done for a wedding cake, but, when it came to it, none of us could eat a thing. So we toasted ourselves with four cups of coffee instead.

To make the day more of an occasion, we went round to see Les' family, to show them the marriage certificate. Her Gran gave us some tea towels, and Aunt Peggy a pink blanket which we use to this day.

When we called on Les' Mum to tell her the news, she said: "Oh, I must buy you a wedding present."

And we're still waiting for that one.

CHAPTER EIGHT

A million-to-one chance that Lesley can have a child.

"**B**EEN MARRIED LONG?" asked a woman as we stood side by side, weighing lumps of cheese in the factory where I had got myself a job.

All day long we cut, weighed and wrapped cheese for supermarkets, and we were supposed to concentrate when we used the scales, because there was trouble if any piece was wrongly priced. But it was so boring working with cheese that we had to have a yarn.

"Six years," I replied, although I had really only been married for six months. I always made out that John and I had been married when we just lived together.

Having a small wedding hadn't bothered me. Just being married was enough, as I had been calling myself Mrs. Brown at the factory before I was entitled to and had been afraid the other women would find out. Now that cheap ring I had worn ever since I ran away with John had gone in the dustbin, as I had a proper one.

"Any children?" asked the woman, as she sliced another wedge of yellow Cheddar.

She was the type who wanted to know everybody's

business, though she'd only worked at the factory for a week.

"A stepdaughter," I said.

"Haven't you started a family of your own?"

"We're not supposed to be chatting while we weigh the cheese," I replied.

Little did that woman dream that having a child was almost all I thought about in that white-tiled factory, while I cut and weighed the cheese. Not getting pregnant had been a worry before I married, but now it was becoming an obsession. It was almost as bad with John.

"Anything happened?" was usually his first question when he got in from work.

Every month since we had been married, I had expected to be pregnant, because my periods were always late. I never got quite as far as looking in baby shops and peeping inside prams, but, as the days went by, the more pregnant I felt.

It was true that I had Sharon, but she had come to me when she was already three. I had never had a baby to look after, and I longed for all those things that mothers usually moan about, like coping with dirty nappies and being kept awake at night.

When I got home from the cheese factory that evening though, John didn't ask his usual question. The look on my face was enough to tell him it hadn't happened again that month. Being married hadn't made any difference, but I suppose I had always known that.

"We just can't go on like this, month after month," John told me. I was always depressed for days after having built up my hopes.

"You're married now. You've every right to find out from the doctor if anything's wrong."

It had to happen, though I dreaded it. I almost knew what the doctor might say.

But that doctor was too busy with a waiting room full of coughing, wheezing patients to give time to a problem like mine.

"You're still very young, Mrs. Brown," he said, scribbling on a pad. I was twenty-two years old and not going to be put off again.

"There is something wrong with me," I said. "And I want to know what it is."

The doctor looked up from his writing pad. Usually he could hardly hear my voice, since I was very shy.

"Alright," he said. "If you insist, I'll send you to the fertility clinic for some tests. That should put your mind at rest."

John picked me up from the clinic in his lorry, because he worried about what I had to go through when I was there. I had always connected hospitals with pain, and inside that clinic, the nurse had to stuff my mouth with cotton wool to stop me screaming out loud while the tests were done. My face was as white as a sheet when John hauled me up beside him in the lorry.

"Let's call all this off, Les. I don't like seeing you looking like this" he said.

But I couldn't do that.

"I'm going to have an operation now," I told him.

"You're an amazing girl, Les," John said. "For someone who'd rather put up with toothache than go to the dentist, I would never have believed you'd go through all this."

The clinic doctor had pumped purple dye through my Fallopian tubes that day to see if they worked. At last they had found out what the trouble was.

"I've got blocked tubes," I told John. It was news to me that I had tubes like these at all. Before all this, I hadn't known much about how babies came about, but I was learning fast.

"I'll never have a baby unless my tubes are un-blocked," I went on.

John looked flabbergasted. "I never thought you'd go into hospital unless you were a stretcher case," he said.

It was true. I had never been a patient in hospital before, and I was scared half to death. But now there wasn't any choice.

The worst time always comes, though, when you least expect it. A few weeks had passed since the operation, and I had to go back to the hospital for a check-up. As it was only routine, I told John not to bother to come along.

But he wanted to. We were so close again that he went everywhere with me. It was his way of sharing what I was going through so we could have our family.

The doctor didn't examine me when I got to the hospital. He sat me in a chair instead, while John waited outside the room.

The doctor wasn't young or old. He just looked like an ordinary bloke. He was probably a family man.

"I'm afraid I've got some bad news, Mrs. Brown." he said. I guessed he was going to tell me I still wasn't pregnant. He had thought I might be shortly after the operation and, although John and I got quite excited, I had secretly thought it was a bit too quick myself.

"The operation wasn't a success," he continued. Oh no, not all that again, I thought, but I still sat looking at him.

"It's a million-to-one chance you'll ever have a baby. There's just nothing we can do to help you," the doctor said.

It was a lot to take in all at once. I still sat there, just looking him. "I'd better fetch your husband," the doctor said.

John stared at my face as the doctor repeated those

words to him. I didn't want to cry in front of the doctor.

"Isn't there anything?" John asked.

"I'm sorry," the doctor replied. He shook us by the hand. Somehow, all along I had known what the doctor had found out. But it was a different matter now it had actually been put into words.

The entrance hall at Bristol General Hospital was as large and gloomy as a railway station, and dozens of people milled around as John and I walked out. Those people were alive, but not me. I felt dead inside.

The road that passed the hospital was a busy one, with heavy trucks and buses hurtling along. A mother with a shiny new pram was waiting at a zebra crossing and, at the sight of her, I broke down.

John wept too, as he put his arms around me. Passers-by stared at us. We must have looked an odd couple, both with tears pouring down our cheeks.

"Come on, let's walk along the river bank," John said. It was a good six miles home, but I was in no state to be seen on a bus.

There was no one down by the river. It was rather like being with John in those early days when I'd run away from Gran's. It felt as if we were all alone in the world. There was no one else like us anywhere.

"It's so unfair," I sobbed. I always had the feeling that if you try hard enough you should get what you want. Didn't I deserve a baby after going through that operation and all those fertility tests?

It had been bad enough as a child, not having proper parents. I had felt different from other people when I was put in a children's home, and, now that I couldn't have a child either, I felt certain that I was.

The trouble was that at that time I didn't know there was anyone else who had to face up to what I had just been told.

Bristol could have been the world, as far as I was concerned. I had lived there all my life, and we never had the money to go for more than a day trip elsewhere. It didn't occur to me that there were thousands of women all over the place who were childless like me.

"I'm not a normal woman," I told John.

"Come off it, luv. You're normal enough for me," he said. As usual, John was the one who was trying to put on a brave face.

We lay in each other's arms in bed that night. Now that it was a million-to-one chance that I'd ever be pregnant, sex was a million miles from our thoughts as well. There wasn't any point any more.

"I wouldn't even blame you now if you went off with someone else," I whispered in the dark. It wasn't John's fault. He could have as many children as he liked with another woman. A whole football team.

"Don't start that again, Les," John said. "The most important thing is that we've still got each other. And we've got Sharon."

But we wouldn't have her for many more years. The flat had seemed so quiet when we got back from hospital, as Sharon had still been at school. Before we knew it, she'd be grown up and leaving home, just as I had done. Yet John and I would still be quite young.

Years of just weighing and packing cheese and coming back to a quiet, empty flat stretched before me. John and I would be so lonely with no child to share and make plans for. There was no future for us any more.

John switched the light on as I started to weep.

"Listen, Les, we've got to get over this," he said. "The doctor said it was a million-to-one chance that we'd have a baby. Well, we're going to make that one chance happen to us.

"We've got to believe that we can have a child."

CHAPTER NINE

Lesley keeps trying to have a child.

CRAZY AS IT sounds, I believed that one-in-a-million chance would happen. That's what kept me going. A part of me wouldn't accept what the hospital doctor had told us. He might have made a mistake.

Once my period was three weeks late, and I was almost certain I was pregnant. As the months became years, I got to expect the disappointments, but they never became less hard to take. It was like being told each month that I would never have a family and I hit rock bottom every time.

"Find yourself a normal woman," I told John whenever I was in the dumps about it. In those days, if someone had told me that John had been seen with another woman, I would have immediately thought he was up to no good again.

It was easier to think the worst of him, in case he left. Then I could tell myself it was what I had expected.

"I've nothing to give our marriage now that I can't have a child," I told him.

"Having children isn't the only reason for being married," John replied. But it seems that way when you can't.

In other ways though, our life had improved. We moved from our flat to a council house in Hassell Drive, where we still live today, and John earned extra money working in a pub at night.

That meant we didn't have to scrimp and save, and we ate meat every night. Not that I remember ever being so hard up that we had to go without anything, except in those early days when we could only afford plates of chips.

John has always been the sort who doesn't spend money on himself. But if Sharon or I wanted anything, we had it, no matter what it was.

If I went out now and blew all we've got, he'd say: "Oh, that's nice." He's daft with money, though it worried me when we were short. I pretended not to be at home when anyone who expected to be paid called at the door.

Buying clothes for myself never interested me much because, still being a terror for sweets, I was usually overweight. But once I set my heart on an imitation leopard skin coat, though goodness knows why. Furs don't suit me because I'm short and fat.

John promised to buy it for me when he got his wages. In those days he didn't earn much more than the £15 the coat cost, so it was back to plates of chips that week.

That coat turned out to be a real waste of money too. It looked so awful on me I only wore it twice.

When the letter arrived to say we had got the council house, Sharon and I behaved like a couple of crazy kids, shouting and dancing round the flat. John was at work, so we rushed down to a neighbour who lived below to tell her the news.

"I wondered what all the noise was about," she said.

I wasn't so grateful when I'd got used to the house though, and I started moaning about not having enough kitchen cupboards and the windows not being big enough. But when we first moved there, it felt wonderful, after all those years living in rooms.

We didn't buy much, as we already had a three-piece suite, a sideboard, a table and some chairs. We changed our black and white television for a colour one, and, being quite good at sewing, I ran up curtains for every room.

"You might as well change your job now we're here," said John, as we got up for work at seven o'clock one morning after settling down in the house. The cheese factory had been just round the corner from our old flat, but now it was half an hour's journey on the bus, and an expensive one at that, since I never earned much.

John looked through the "Situations Vacant" page in the newspaper. Machinists were wanted. "You're a trained machinist," he said. "You'd get more money."

"I'll think about it," I told him. I didn't like being rushed.

The windows at the cheese factory were so high up that we couldn't see the sky. All there was to look at were cold, white tiles. There were fifty-pound blocks of cheese to hump around, though all that work we once did by hand is coped with by a machine today.

A few women had already started slicing the cheese when I got to work. Some of those factory women were real bitches. They always found the worst to say about everybody else.

"Mavis is bringing in her baby today," one said. Mavis had worked there before she had her first child.

The other women glanced at me. They seemed

embarrassed talking about babies in front of me, since I had told them that I couldn't have any children.

"Mavis looks a right mess these days," the woman continued. "No money, I suppose. Her old man's on the club."

I always dreaded anyone at the factory getting pregnant or coming around to show off their babies to the rest of us. I wouldn't say I was jealous, because that's too harsh a word, and I was glad for those girls. But they never realised how much I envied them as well.

I wasn't religious, but sometimes I said a little prayer: "Dear God, I wouldn't moan about being kept awake at night and washing dirty nappies if you'd let me have a child."

We got up to silly games in the factory to make the time pass, and one was "I Spy", which we played until Mavis turned up just before dinner time.

Everyone gathered round to look at the baby, and Mavis had put on quite a show. Even the baby's booties were covered in frills, and she was plump and rosy-cheeked herself. She didn't look a mess at all.

"Do you mind not being able to have a kid?" one woman asked me. Everyone seemed to stare at me.

"As I can't, I don't think about it," I replied.

At last Mavis and her baby disappeared to the canteen with the other women. I had two good friends at the factory and they stayed behind with me. They probably guessed how I really felt.

On the bus home, I thought about changing my job. It would mean new faces, and questions about how many children I'd got. At least I had got used to the women where I was.

"I'm sticking to my job," I told John when I got indoors. He didn't bother to argue with me once I had made up my mind.

John rushed his tea to get off to work at the pub. It didn't seem fair, as he had already put in a full day's work driving his lorry. I wished he'd give up that pub job. Being on my own meant I had time to think, and in those days, I only seemed to have one subject on my mind.

When John left, I got out a medical book that I had borrowed from the library. I read anything I could find about getting pregnant, and I watched out for programmes about it on the television.

What often worried me was that I might have done something that had caused the trouble with my Fallopian tubes. I had gone over all the illnesses I had ever had to try and find a reason for it. It didn't seem right that I had been born with blocked tubes.

"It's just one of those things," John told me. "It's not your fault. It's ridiculous to go through life blaming yourself."

John and I also talked about adoption, and we had even gone to the Children's Committee, which I had been under as a child, not having a father or much to do with Mum. I remember Aunt Peggy taking me along to their offices to get an allowance for a new school uniform, so I thought I might stand a good chance since I was already known there.

But they didn't even bother to put down our names. There weren't enough babies to go round, what with abortion and women being on the pill, and anyway, the committee preferred regular churchgoers to people like us.

"Have you thought of becoming foster parents?" asked a woman from the Children's Committee, when she saw I was upset.

But that would have been no good. I could never have parted from a child once I had looked after it. It would have felt like mine, just as Sharon did. Right from the first day I had her, she had always been my little girl.

It was nearly midnight when I shut the medical book, which hadn't told me anything that I didn't already know by heart. John usually got in about that time after clearing up at the pub.

My feelings for John had changed that day at the hospital when we heard the worst. Everything seemed different afterwards when we got back to the flat. I had never felt so close to John. He was all I had, the only one who understood what I was going through, because he felt the same himself.

We still had ups and downs, but they never lasted long. John had a quick temper, which was over in a minute. It flared up when I went on at him. "Nag, nag, nag," he said. "Leave me alone, can't you?"

My own temper had disappeared. I got into moods instead. But even in the blackest ones, I didn't really expect him to walk out, no matter what I said. Just the fact that he was still around seemed to mean he always would be. I thought that it would be just John and me forever.

The backroom clock said half past twelve. John was never normally as late back from the pub as that. It crossed my mind that he'd had an accident. It was at times like that when I realised how much I needed him.

His key turned in the front door. "Sorry luv," John said. He looked worn out, but there was another expression on his face. It reminded me of his look when I noticed that love bite on his neck.

"Don't be daft," I told myself. "You're imagining things again."

"I don't want to see another dirty beer glass in my life," said John, pulling off his shoes.

"Why not pack it in?" I asked. It wouldn't matter if we were hard up again. John always said we'd manage, and we always did.

"That landlord's a nice bloke," he replied. "I can't let him down at such a busy time." I had only been to the pub where John worked a few times. Once we had taken Gran along to have a port and lemon.

It seemed like any other pub to me, but John seemed to like it there.

A few weeks later, I came across a letter as I was sorting out the dirty clothes. John never put his clothes straight into the washing basket. He just left his socks and underpants lying about the bedroom floor, and it made me mad.

As I emptied one of his trouser pockets the letter fell out.

"Dear John," it said. It ended with lots of love from Jane.

CHAPTER TEN

John's luck changes.

JANE REALLY HANDED herself to me on a plate. She was a sexy bit as well. She had an enormous bust, but she never wore a bra.

She worked part time at the pub, and we got chatting when I was moved from the lounge to serving in the public bar.

Pulling pints was much more in my line than pouring gin and tonics for those snobby, lounge bar types, though barristers, solicitors and even private dentists also drank in the public bar. I often had a good laugh with them, since they weren't stuck up at all.

"Where's your boyfriend tonight?" I asked Jane. She was a pretty girl, so it was surprising to find she hadn't got a bloke.

"I don't go out much," she said.

It was pelting down with rain that night, so I gave Jane a lift home. I had an old, second-hand car at that time. When we reached Jane's flat, she asked me in to have a cup of coffee.

There didn't seem any harm in that. Jane came from

quite a well-off family in Haywards Heath. Her father was an engineer, working on a hydro-electric dam in South Africa, and Jane had the run of the house when she was home, because her mother was always out doing work for the W.V.S.

Jane had come to Bristol to work in a travel agency. "Someday I'll be a courier and travel all over the world," she said.

"Won't your parents mind?" I asked. Jane was very young. She couldn't have been more than twenty at the time.

"My parents let me do what I like. They're very broadminded," she replied. "We don't even have a lock on the bathroom door, so my father just wanders in when I'm in the bath. He never bothers if I see him with nothing on as well."

That really shocked me. I wouldn't have behaved like that with my daughter Sharon, and she was only ten. Well-off people seemed to have a whole different set of morals from a bloke like me.

"How did you make out with Jane?" another barman, who was also called John, asked as soon as I arrived at the pub next evening.

"She's a funny bird," I said. "Do you know, she lets her dad see her in the bath."

"You're alright there, you randy devil," said John, giving me a nudge.

Suddenly it dawned on me why Jane had told me that. No more lifts home for her, I thought. Les still hadn't got over Janet, and I wasn't going to risk everything for another bit of skirt.

There was a commotion in the public bar a few nights later when the locals arrived to make a protest. What had got them steamed up was the noise made by the cars that pulled up outside the pub when a darts match was going on, and they demanded that the darts board be taken down.

Arguing was thirsty work, and we were rushed off our feet until closing time, when nothing had been decided and the darts board was still hanging on the wall.

"Come on," I said to Jane, after we had washed the umpteenth glass. It didn't seem fair to let her walk home when I had the car.

"Coffee?" she asked, as I pulled up outside her flat.

"Better not. It's late," I said. Jane's sweater was very tight. I was sorely tempted to go up to her flat.

"Well, we'd better say goodnight," she said, and she leant her head on my shoulder.

After that, it wasn't so much what she said as what she did to me. If Les had behaved in the same way, she would have had her clothes off in two seconds flat.

Jane was getting me in a terrible state. My hand strayed towards that tight jumper of hers, and then I stopped. Just like a car engine, I switched off. My conscience wouldn't let me go any further.

"It looks as if I'd better be going," Jane said with a sigh. "Another time perhaps?"

I was already kicking myself as she got out of the car. I must have been mad, turning down the opportunity with a cracker like that.

"I warned you. I said that I'd leave if you started messing about again with some other woman."

Les ranted and raved about the kitchen, and I couldn't understand at first what she was on about, since several weeks had passed since that fumble with Jane.

Les threw a letter onto the kitchen table. "What's all this about?" she cried. I had forgotten all about Jane's letter in my trouser pocket.

Jane had got herself a free ticket from her travel

bureau to visit the holy places in Israel. "Don't forget to send me a postcard," I had joked when she left.

Since that night in the car, I hadn't given Jane a lift home on her own. I was only human, and I didn't know how I'd behave given a second chance.

"She's just a girl who worked in the pub," I told Les. "I gave her a lift home once or twice, but that's all. I never laid a hand on her. I've nothing to reproach myself for."

But, since Les didn't believe me anyway, I might as well have had.

"Why does she say that she misses you?"

Les seemed to have learnt that letter off by heart, and a pretty sexy one it was too. Jane hadn't spent much time at those holy places by the sound of it.

"Perhaps she did fancy me," I said. "But she's the sort who would fancy anything in trousers. You read the letter, didn't you? You can tell what she's like."

Les cooled down a bit. "I don't like you working at that pub," she said.

Les still didn't trust me. After letting her down with Janet all that time ago, I could understand that.

"Alright," I told her. "I'll pack it in. Anyway, I'm fed up working at nights."

We settled down after that and, on the face of it, we did alright for ourselves. We saved up for a deposit to buy our council house and we had our own car. Each year we also managed a two-week holiday in a caravan at Swanage.

The railway money wasn't fantastic. I had to work seven days a week to pay our way. The most I could afford to drink was half a pint in the off-sales when I went to buy a packet of cigarettes. In those days I was known as "half-pint Johnny" at the local pub. I enjoyed a drink, but I couldn't even afford to go out for a pint at Sunday dinner time.

Our weeks were pretty full though. Every Friday, if the season was right, we went to speedway meetings, and, once a week, we saw Les' Gran. There was another evening every week at Les' cousin Judith's house, and she and her husband returned our visit each Thursday. So practically every evening was accounted for.

When I left at five o'clock in the morning to drive my lorry, Les was often moaning about getting up to go all the way to the cheese factory. Why she was still there was a mystery, but Les has always had a mind of her own.

When she said something, that was it. Arguing was a waste of time. If Les said the moon was blue and I insisted it was yellow, I'd have to give in eventually. I've yet to beat her when she makes up her mind about anything.

She was often moody in those days and, though we seldom talked about it any longer, I knew what she was brooding about. You'd think, as the years passed, it would have become easier to accept that we weren't going to have a family. But it never was.

When people asked, I tried to make out it wasn't so bad for me, having had a family in my first marriage and Sharon being my own child. But that wasn't how I really felt. I wanted a family just as much as Les. She was my wife, and I wanted her to have my baby. It would have made all the difference in the world to have our own child.

Why us? I often thought. It just didn't seem fair.

Sometimes Les went quiet for days. Her face became a mask, and I felt almost too scared to talk to her. I knew what was going on in her mind, but there was nothing I could do to help her.

"Coming up to bed?" I asked her one night.

"Not yet. I want to watch this programme on the telly."

She always made the same excuse. Les stayed up so late that our sex life had really gone to pot.

Sometimes, as I lay in bed, struggling to stay awake until she came up, I almost lost my temper. I felt like rushing downstairs and dragging her to bed. It seemed as if she stayed up on purpose so we couldn't make love.

But I was determined that she wouldn't get away with it that night. I had worked out the best time of the month for Les to get pregnant, and this was it. Saving myself up for that one night a month was quite exciting, but I never let on to Les. If we both knew what was going on, it would have taken all the feeling out of making love.

To my mind, Les had given up hoping for that one-in-a-million chance. But I've always been an optimist. Les looked surprised when I picked up the newspaper instead of turning in. I flicked through the pages. However exhausted I felt, I wasn't going to lose this chance.

There was a story in the paper about a couple who had ill-treated their child. It almost broke my heart to think people like that could have babies, and not us.

Just passing a baby in its pram was bad enough. Les never said anything, but I knew how she felt, because it cut me up inside as well.

Les' television programme finished. There was nothing else to watch. Les couldn't sit there looking at a dot on the screen. She had to come to bed with me.

She hung about in the bathroom for long enough while I lay waiting. There were old wives' tales about getting pregnant that we had heard about, such as making love upside down and knocking Les' head four times on the bedroom wall afterwards, but we hadn't gone in for that sort of thing.

Les had never been a great one for experimenting

with sex and, though I had often thought of catching her in the shower, I had never had the guts to try. Knowing Les, she'd have probably kicked me straight out.

"Leave off," she said, as I put my arms around her in bed. Being rejected made me feel as clumsy as a carthorse, but I had to keep trying that night. It might just work this time.

"How are you ever going to get pregnant when we never make love?" I asked, as Les turned her back on me.

"I won't anyway," she muttered. "You'll have to find yourself a proper woman."

If she said that once more, I'd shake her and tell her to buck up her own ideas or that's exactly what I'd do. Sometimes I wondered how I stuck it. At moments like that, there just didn't seem any point in being together any more.

But I couldn't hurt Les. She had suffered enough, not being able to have a child.

"Why don't you go back to that fertility clinic?" I said. "They might be able to help you now."

New discoveries were being made every day, and several years had passed since we'd been to the clinic.

"After all," I went on. "Scientists have put a spaceman on the moon." Compared to that, making Les pregnant seemed such a little thing.

"I've wanted to go to the clinic for ages, but I'm scared," she replied. "What if the doctor says there's no hope again?"

"I'll come with you, Les," I said.

She turned towards me and I stroked her hair. "We mustn't give up," I whispered. I didn't know what would become of us if we did.

Les had softened now. I took her in my arms again.

"Come on, missus," I said. "Let's try to have a baby in our own way. One more time for luck."

There was a woman called Dr. Hinton who had done those tests on Les seven years before at the clinic, and it was she who saw us again.

"I'm afraid there is still nothing this clinic can do for you," she said. Les' face was becoming a mask again.

The doctor hesitated, as if she wasn't sure if she should go on.

"There is a doctor in Oldham called Mr. Steptoe, who has done a lot of research into the problem of blocked tubes," she said slowly.

"What he's doing sounds almost like science fiction. He's trying to develop ways of helping women with damaged tubes to conceive a baby.

"He might be able to help you."

Les was already looking excited. "How can we get in touch with him?" I asked.

"Mr. Brown, it would be a big risk to take," Dr. Hinton said. "It might mean you'd have to live in Oldham for several months so your wife could be treated by Mr. Steptoe.

"You'd have to move house, leave your job, and it would probably be all for nothing. I don't believe Mr. Steptoe has had any success with his method yet."

I didn't have to look at Les again. "We'll try anything," I said.

"We'll sell the car, the house even, if it comes to it," I told Les, as we walked away from the clinic. My arm was around her. There was nothing I wouldn't give up if it meant we could have a child. Suddenly we had hope in our life.

We went on our caravan holiday, still waiting to hear from Mr. Steptoe. Perhaps we should have saved the money in the circumstances, but we enjoyed those times at Swanage. After doing a job fifty weeks a year, to my mind every working man deserves a two-week holiday. The caravan only cost us £20 anyway, as it was owned by a bloke at work.

Saturday afternoon came in the caravan and, as usual, I checked my football pools coupon. No good, I thought, and chucked the coupon in the bin. But then I had second thoughts and fished out the screwed-up piece of paper, spread it out in front of me and took another look.

"Nine draws!" I hollered. "I've won the pools!"

"Don't be daft," said Les. "You say the same thing every week."

It was true that each Saturday I thought my coupon was a winner. But this time I had got nine out of sixteen draws. About £45 to come, or so I calculated.

As usual, we only had enough money at the end of the holiday for petrol home, but that never mattered. There's no point in going away if you don't go a bit wild. So, broke as usual, we picked up the pile of bills that waited for us on the doormat.

One letter contained a cheque for £800, which I couldn't make head or tail of at all, so I put it on one side while I sorted through the rest of the mail.

Suddenly it dawned on me. That massive cheque was my pools win. I couldn't believe it was so much. I'd never had so much money in my life.

Les was holding a letter from Mr. Steptoe. "He wants to see me," she said.

"Well, we can afford to go now," I replied. I hugged Les. "Winning the pools is just the start. We're going to have a baby as well.

"Our luck has really changed."

CHAPTER ELEVEN

Lesley meets Mr. Steptoe, the gynaecologist.

WE LEFT BRISTOL at the crack of dawn for our appointment with Mr. Steptoe. It was to be at 3.15 in the afternoon in his consulting rooms in Manchester.

His letter had fixed a date four months in advance, and it had been so bad hanging about for so long that we didn't want to be a minute late when the day arrived.

It was a long train journey, but we weren't on a joy ride. We were going to see about having a family, so it didn't matter how far we had to go.

John had been wrong about me giving up hope. After all those years of not getting pregnant, it would have sounded daft if I had kept going on about it, but it was still what I thought about most of the time.

From my reading and from watching television programmes, I knew that doctors had made a lot of medical advances. They had even tried giving women plastic Fallopian tubes when their own were blocked, and I wondered if a pair of those might help me.

It had been on my mind for ages to get in touch with

the fertility clinic again. When my cousin Judith came round and told us she was pregnant, I almost rushed straight to the clinic the next morning to ask the doctor to make the same thing happen to me. Enough money was spent on contraceptives and abortions so that women didn't have to have children. It seemed about time that they helped someone to have a baby as well.

But it still took a push from John to get me back to the clinic. What always stopped me was the thought of what the doctor might say. I didn't want to be told again that there was still nothing that could be done.

In all my reading on the subject, I had never come across Mr. Steptoe's name. But when Dr. Hinton asked if we would like her to write to him on our behalf, I didn't hesitate. "Oh, yes please," I said.

That one-in-a-million chance wasn't going to happen to John and me on our own.

It was a freezing November day when the train pulled into Manchester. The air in Bristol seemed bad enough, but it could have blown in from paradise compared to the smutty stuff up there.

St. John Street, where Mr. Steptoe had his offices, was full of specialists, just like London's Harley Street, so we didn't expect it to be difficult to find.

But when we asked a railway porter how to get there, he spoke in such a thick accent we couldn't understand a word. Even the street directory didn't help. The list of streets wouldn't correspond to where they were supposed to be on the map.

"Someone's bound to know outside the station," John said. There was an old man huddled up on a windy corner, selling religious pamphlets. John fished in his pocket for ten pence. We had to buy a pamphlet before the man told us the way.

"And a lot of rubbish he told us, too," moaned

John, as we walked round and round the same streets. "That bloke just wanted to sell us one of his religious books."

It started to rain. It streaked down the dirty buildings that were so unfamiliar and drab. People who hurried past all looked the same. No one seemed to want to stop and help us.

It felt as if we had walked all over Manchester by the time we found a police station, but even that wasn't like any I'd ever been inside. There was no desk, no policemen around, just a telephone stuck on a plain, brick wall.

It was just after midday, only three hours away from our appointment with Mr. Steptoe. For all we knew, his rooms might be just round the corner. But if we didn't find them soon, we might even be too late to see him.

A policeman appeared as if from nowhere as soon as John picked up the telephone. "What are you up to?" he yelled, standing in a doorway on the other side of the empty, brick-walled room.

"We've just come in for a bit of information," John said. He was as red as if he'd been caught with his fingers in the till. Everyone seemed so unfriendly. Even the policeman was carrying on as if we were up to no good.

"Don't bother yourself," John said. "You can stuff your information if you can't be more civil to us."

John must have been really narked to have talked to a copper like that, but it did the trick. The policeman cooled down a bit. "St. John Street's just round the corner, past the hospital. Who are you going to see there?" he asked.

"Mr. Steptoe," John told him. Trust us to have been on top of the street all the time.

The rain had turned into sleet by the time we stood outside Mr. Steptoe's offices. Even John was feeling the cold, and he had on his heavy overcoat.

We couldn't just stand outside, as there was still over two hours to go. But now that we knew where Mr. Steptoe was, it was safe enough to find a cafe. So we had a plate of egg and chips.

We even did some Christmas shopping. We had brought £60, which was our Christmas savings, and I looked round Marks & Spencers for a cardigan for Gran. But everything seemed much more expensive up there, so we didn't buy a thing.

John showed the letter Mr. Steptoe had sent us to the woman who opened his door. It was exactly three o'clock. Fifteen minutes to go.

The people in the waiting room were toffed up to the eyebrows. Being private patients, they were a posh lot. Since we had come so far, I hadn't dressed myself up, and we must both have looked a sight after tramping round Manchester all day in the rain. A woman in a fur coat stared at us as if we were as common as muck.

"Well, come in," said Mr. Steptoe. His voice sounded very abrupt. He was an elderly man and he wore a dark striped suit. He didn't seem a nasty bloke but, being such a high-up, important doctor, I assumed he was rather hard and cold.

"Have you had your semen tested?" he asked John.

"Eh?" John spluttered. He was shaking in his boots.

"Your sperm," Mr. Steptoe said, a bit impatiently.

"Oh, that. The clinic tested it. I didn't understand that other word," John replied.

Mr. Steptoe gave me a short examination on the couch. "Your ovaries don't seem blocked," he murmured. "You're twenty-nine, aren't you, Mrs. Brown?"

My age worried me a lot. Each birthday meant another year had gone by without a baby. Though thirty wasn't very old, it seemed that way when I still hadn't had a child. I'd soon be too old for childbearing if I didn't hurry up.

"Don't worry. You're just the right age for my purpose," Mr. Steptoe told me. "Not too young or too old. I wouldn't have been able to help you if you'd been over thirty-six." Thank goodness I'd come in time.

"I'll have to do a little operation if you want to go ahead with this," Mr. Steptoe said. "It will mean making a small cut to put an instrument inside you, so I can have a close look at the state of your Fallopian tubes.

"You'll have to be prepared for a second operation if I'm to do the implant."

He looked at both of us from behind his desk. "Do you understand what an implant means?" he asked.

John and I shook our heads. I hadn't really understood what the clinic doctor had explained. All I had grasped was that it might make me pregnant.

Mr. Steptoe told us that he would take an egg from my ovaries and it would be fertilised by John's sperm. Then, a couple of days later, the fertilised egg would be planted back inside me to grow into a baby.

It meant being in hospital a lot, but that couldn't be helped.

Those places still scared the life out of me, but I was more scared of not having a child.

"Are you ready to make a decision now?" Mr. Steptoe asked.

Little did he know just how prepared we were. As soon as we had got Mr. Steptoe's letter, John had been down to the Council offices to ask about our mortgage repayments if we had to move to Oldham for six months. When he explained why we were going there, the Council official agreed not to send any demand letters for our mortgage while we were away. We would have to pay two monthly instalments every month when we got back.

It had been more difficult to get John off his job. The railway welfare officer said it was impossible to transfer him to Manchester or Oldham for so short a time. So John asked our doctor if, in the circumstances, he could go on welfare for six months.

"I can't do that, when there's nothing wrong with you," the doctor replied. But he said he would try and get us a supplementary benefit from the Social Security instead.

The railway agreed to give John leave of absence for six months. We were all ready to move up to Oldham at once.

"It can't be done that quickly, I'm afraid," said Mr. Steptoe and he almost smiled. "You'll have to wait until there's a place for you in the hospital. I'll phone you when you can be fitted in."

But we hadn't got a phone. We gave him the number of my cousin Judith, because we saw a lot of her.

"You won't be lonely in hospital," said Mr. Steptoe, as he walked us to the door. "You won't be on your own. You'll be with girls who are going through exactly what's going to happen to you."

My impression of Mr. Steptoe had been wrong. He wasn't cold and hard at all. He couldn't be, if he understood a little about how I felt.

"Will you settle up now, Mr. Brown?" asked the woman who had let us in.

I wondered what she was on about. Everything had been on the National Health before.

"That will be £25," she said. Our mouths almost dropped open. It had felt as if we'd only been two minutes in Mr. Steptoe's room. It was going to be an expensive baby at that rate.

It turned out that I had to be a private patient, or I would have to wait a year or two on the National Health for the operation Mr. Steptoe had to carry out. I wasn't getting any younger, so there was no time to lose.

"I told you that pools win changed our luck," said John as we walked back to the railway station. It wasn't sleeting any more. John was holding my hand, and a woman smiled at us as we waited to cross the road. Manchester wasn't such a bad place after all.

That eight hundred pounds wouldn't go far. Before our pools win, John had been saving for us moving to Oldham by driving a taxi at night. He could always do that again.

We would find the money somehow, even if it meant selling the house. Whatever happened, it would work out. This baby was meant to be.

I don't remember Mr. Steptoe saying his method of producing babies had ever worked, and I certainly didn't ask. I just imagined that hundreds of children had already been born through being conceived outside their mothers' wombs.

Having a baby was all that mattered. It didn't seem strange that I had never read about anyone who had had a child in that way before. I could understand their mothers wanting to keep quiet afterwards about how their children had been started off.

It just didn't occur to me that it would almost be a miracle if it worked with me. I wouldn't have believed it if Mr. Steptoe had told me straight out that, after years of trying, no one had ever had a baby from an implant.

My mind was made up. "I'll soon be pregnant now," I told myself on the train home.

CHAPTER TWELVE

Lesley has her first operation.

I T WAS CALLED A laparoscopy, which meant putting a tiny camera inside to see what was wrong with me.

All I seemed to do in the three months before there was a bed at the hospital was to wait for that phone call from Mr. Steptoe. Yet, when John and I arrived at our lodgings in Oldham the night before the operation, I would have almost been glad if the whole thing had been put off.

It was freezing in the boarding house, and I got into bed in my nightdress, dressing gown and a pair of John's socks. But I was cold more from fear of what was to happen the next day.

John didn't say a lot either, as he must have guessed I was in a state. Even though he was beside me, I felt so alone as I lay awake that night.

Early the following morning, we walked up the hill that led to Oldham General Hospital. It was winter in a strange, bleak town and no one was about. We passed open spaces, with buildings flattened by bulldozers or bombs, and great empty mills, still standing, with their windows smashed, leaving dark, gaping holes like wounds.

John took my hand. We knew what we had to do, so there wasn't a lot to say.

Mr. Steptoe only made a tiny incision, nothing really to have got worked up about. He wanted me to remain in hospital an extra day, as the wound hadn't quite closed. But we couldn't afford to stay in Oldham for more than one night after the operation.

The wound started to bleed as soon as we got on the train home. It was only covered by a little bandage and there was a four-hour journey ahead of us.

"Blast it," said John. "Working on the railways, I should have known better than to put us next to the baggage compartment." That meant a jerky journey and I was in agony at every jolt.

Blood began to soak through my underclothes. It felt as if the wound had opened right up, and the thought of that frightened me half to death.

"Is your wife alright?" asked an old lady sitting next to John.

"Not really. She had an operation yesterday. She shouldn't be travelling, but she wanted to come home."

"She looks so white," said the old dear. She offered me her battery-operated fan to revive me, but I didn't want to make a fuss.

The blood started to seep through my thick woollen dress. I held my coat tightly around me, so no one would see.

We changed trains four times on the journey to Bristol, and at one station, I was crying so much that John picked me up and carried me in his arms from one end of the platform to the next. It must have been about a quarter of a mile. John was so upset about the state I was in that he was crying too.

The car was parked at Bristol Temple Meads Station, and he laid me in the back. People blasted their horns, as cars and lorries piled up behind us, while John crept along so I wouldn't feel any more jolts.

"Belt up," he yelled back at those motorists.

He laid me on the settee in the backroom and opened my coat. Tears poured down his face at the sight of all that blood. With a bowl of hot water and Dettol, he bathed my clothes.

"That's it. No more," John said. "You're not going back to that hospital again."

I sat on the settee in my nightdress, a new dressing on the wound. It hadn't been nearly as bad as I had thought. The wound hadn't really opened much at all.

"I'm not going through another experience like that," John continued. "Even having a baby doesn't make it worth suffering so much."

He seemed determined. But so was I.

"There's no way you'll make me give up," I told him. "As soon as Mr. Steptoe wants me again, I'm going straight back."

Dr. Kershaw's Cottage Hospital, where I had the implant, is just a little place in Royton, a suburb of Oldham, with two private rooms at either end of a big ward. There were two other girls called Sue and Jean who were having an implant at the same time as me. Sue shared a room with me, while Jean was in the other one on her own.

No one in the big ward was supposed to know what was happening to the three of us. Mr. Steptoe had warned us not to tell anyone why we were there. We pretended we were having fertility tests, which we were in a way.

John was due at the hospital one morning at nine o'clock. Half an hour before nine, I was already watching at the french windows in my room for his car. He had to drive all the way from Bristol, and it would be terrible if he was late, because this was such an important day.

I had already been into the operating theatre. There an egg had been removed from my ovaries. Now it was John's turn. He had to fertilise the egg to make it grow into a child, and he had to be on time for that.

I had almost thought that I wasn't going to get this far. After being the first of the three of us to arrive at the hospital, I became the last to be taken for the operation. Sue and Jean had been to the operating theatre while I waited to be fetched. After a few days, I was in a real panic on the phone to John. It seemed as if I wasn't going to be given the chance after all.

But, as it turned out, it was just my body's fault. I was later in reaching a state of ovulation than the other girls.

Sue had a smile all over her face when she came back from the theatre. I didn't have to ask her if it had been a success. But when Jean returned, she was breaking her heart.

"They can't do anything for me," she cried. "They couldn't get an egg."

I put my arms around her, but there was nothing I could say. The same thing might happen to me. I knew exactly how she must have felt.

"We nearly gave up with you, too," Mr. Steptoe told me after I had had my turn. It had been so hard to get an egg from me that at one point Mr. Steptoe had given up. It was his colleague, Dr. Edwards, who persuaded him to have another try. "And we finally managed it," he told me.

"It's a good job you did," I thought.

John's car screeched into the hospital forecourt.

"So you got here alright," I cried, rushing out.

"Only just," John replied. "I nearly killed myself getting here. I drove like a bloody maniac to be on time."

He had only had an hour's sleep because he'd left Bristol in the night. I hoped he was in a fit state to manage what he had to do.

It was just three minutes to nine. "I told you a lie," I said. "You're not really needed until eleven o'clock, but I told you to come earlier as I was so afraid you'd be late."

"I could murder you, missus," John said, and then he hugged me. He seemed excited too. "I hope this baby of ours is going to be worth all this."

Fourteen days passed after the implant. As soon as the fertilised egg had been put back inside me, I felt pregnant. But Sue was in a different frame of mind.

Each morning, when she woke up in the bed next to mine, she said: "I know it's not going to work."

"For goodness sake, shut up," I replied. "That's not the right attitude to take."

But she couldn't stop worrying. We were supposed to rest in bed for twelve hours each day, but Sue was trying so hard to be pregnant that she stayed there almost all the time.

She wouldn't even have a bath, though I took one every day. To my mind, a little warm water wasn't going to do any harm if I was meant to be pregnant. I had given up smoking though, as that was what expectant mothers were supposed to do.

"Didn't you hear the nurses say it hadn't worked on anyone before?" Sue was carrying on again.

I had been so excited after the implant, believing I was pregnant, that the nurses had reminded me of that too.

"Don't make up your mind," the sister told me. "Mr. Steptoe hasn't had one success so far."

She was being kind, so that I wouldn't be too disappointed, but I wouldn't listen. Mr. Steptoe had warned me in the same way, but, stupid as it sounds, I wouldn't even believe him. This was my last chance. There was no other way I could become pregnant now, since Mr. Steptoe had already done an operation to remove my Fallopian tubes. This had to work.

"Don't take any notice," I told Sue. "They're only telling us that because all the babies born from implants have been kept secret. After all, we've already been told not to let on why we're here."

The next morning, Sue didn't say anything when she woke up. She was a long time in the bathroom and, when she came out, she said, "It hasn't worked. I've started a period."

"Maybe it's nothing," I said.

"Oh, yes, it is," she replied. I expected her to break down, but she didn't even cry. She went into the corridor to tell the staff nurse.

I had become close to Sue after all the hours we'd spent together. Having imagined for so long that I was the only one in existence who couldn't have a baby, it had been amazing to meet someone in the same position as me. Now I realised there were hundreds, maybe thousands, of women who had had to face the same problem as me.

Time sped by in our hospital room, as there was always so much for Sue and me to talk about. We shared all the same feelings about being childless, and, when we got our babies, we planned to visit each other regularly. Being the same age, our children were bound to be friends.

The staff nurse put her arms round Sue, and they walked back to our room.

"I'm so sorry, Sue," I said.

Sue was only twenty-seven. She could try an implant again. But it wasn't the moment to tell her that. There were no words that would have helped.

She was very quiet that day, and early the next morning she left. She hadn't cried at all. But when she had gone, I broke down myself.

Now I was alone in the room. There were still a few days to go for me, as I had had the implant after Sue. It was just a matter of taking one day at a time. Every day was another one gone. Even passing the date didn't mean much, as my periods never were on time.

The other patients in the big ward were a nosey lot. There was one woman who kept asking questions about whether I was pregnant. So I preferred to stay in my room and eat my meals on my own.

John still had his job in Bristol. He was saving his leave of absence for the later months, so he could only come up to see me at weekends. He left me a portable television, but I didn't watch it much. I couldn't concentrate on anything except what was happening inside me.

Mr. Steptoe dropped in every day. He always wanted to know if I had any problems. But the only one I had he couldn't do anything about. All we could do was wait and see, and the days dragged on.

Though I believe in God, I'm not the sort who often prays. I always start when things aren't going too well or I want something, and I had never wanted anything more than to have a baby.

So I started to pray. Each night, I shut my eyes as I sat up in bed.

"Please God, answer this prayer," I said.

CHAPTER THIRTEEN

John becomes an expectant father.

A LETTER ARRIVED FROM Dr. Edwards, Mr. Steptoe's colleague, just before Christmas, when Les
had been home from hospital for about a week.
He wrote to say that she wasn't allowed to do any
skiing, horse riding or Christmas shopping, as her pregnancy test had proved positive. The neighbours must
have wondered what all the racket was about as I danced
around the house, waving the letter in my hand. Then it
struck me where Les was.

That daft missus of mine was down in the town
doing the Christmas shopping, the very thing Dr.
Edwards had told her not to do. Luckily, she had never
been skiing or on a horse in her life, so I didn't have that
to worry about as well.

Mr. Steptoe hadn't committed himself about Les
being pregnant when she left hospital. It was now six
weeks after the implant, but she had it on her mind
that perhaps she still hadn't had a period because she'd
been thinking so much about it.

"You're pregnant," I cried, flying out of the house,

as Les turned the corner of our road. I grabbed the two heavy shopping baskets from her hands.

"You stupid cow," I yelled. "You're not supposed to do any Christmas shopping. You're not going skiing either."

"What are you on about?" Les asked.

Les had probably had just as good an idea as I had that she was pregnant, though neither of us had admitted it. We hadn't wanted to build up our hopes for nothing once again.

"I feel like getting sloshed," I said, after Les had read Dr. Edwards' letter.

"Oh, no, you don't," she replied. "We mustn't count our chickens too soon."

We had a quiet Christmas. Instead of having the whole family over, as we usually do, it was just Les, Sharon and me. On Christmas Day, I follow the same tradition as my Dad by cooking the dinner myself and having a drink with the neighbours beforehand.

The turkey was in the oven when we popped next door to our neighbours, Mary and John. John poured me a beer. Les said she'd have a Babycham, and I felt like blurting out: "Not too much for the missus. She's pregnant, you know."

But I kept my mouth shut. As Les said, it was early days yet. We were still afraid something might go wrong.

Mary and John's three little boys were playing with their new toys on the backroom floor. Sharon was seventeen, too old for presents like that. But it wasn't all over for us. What a Christmas we would have next year, opening our baby's presents under the tree.

Les looked pale when she finished her drink. "We'd better be getting back," she said. She never liked letting others know when she wasn't feeling herself.

As soon as she got indoors, she threw up. "That's a good sign," I muttered to myself, as I basted the turkey.

After dinner, the telly went on the blink and Les was sick again. But it was a fantastic day for all that.

Boxing Day, though, was a different matter. Les was cooking dinner, while I fiddled with the telly, trying to get a decent picture. From the corner of my eye, I spotted a dog from across the road making a mess on our back garden lawn. Even Sheltie, our own dog, wasn't allowed to do that, so I grabbed this mutt by the scruff of its neck and belted it over the fence.

But that didn't teach it a lesson. It was only a little dog, but every time I chucked it out of the garden, it wriggled back under the fence again.

"Dinner's nearly ready," called Les. By that time, I'd really got my hair up. If it was the last thing I did, I was determined to fix that blasted dog.

"Hang on," I told Les, as I belted upstairs. There had to be something to block up the hole in the fence where the dog kept getting through. I grabbed a wooden-framed mattress that we used as a spare bed, and hacked at the frame with a saw, which a relative had given me that Christmas.

With every stroke of the saw, I cursed that dog. "If I get my hands on it again, it will be its head that I'll saw off," I told myself.

So furiously was I cutting the wood, that I didn't notice my finger was in the way. I almost sawed the top of it right off.

Blood poured over the bedroom carpet. I could imagine what Les would say when she saw the mess.

Holding on to the top of my finger, I tried to work out what to do. Les mustn't find out how bad the cut was. In her state, it wouldn't do for her to get upset.

Sharon was in the bath, so I knocked softly on the door. "Cover yourself up," I whispered through the key-hole. "I'm coming in."

"What's up, Dad?" asked Sharon, sitting in the bath with a towel over her. Blood poured over the floor as I rummaged through the bathroom cabinet for something to hold the top of my finger in place.

"Get out of that bath," I told her. "And don't make a fuss in front of Les. You'll have to come to hospital with me. I've nearly cut my finger off."

By that time, I could really have murdered that bloody dog.

Les was dishing up the dinner. "That will have to wait," I told her. She went white when she saw my finger. Les never could stand the sight of blood.

"Don't get het up," I said. "It's not much of a cut, but it's a bit deep. I think I'll just pop down to the hospital to get it stitched up."

When I got back from hospital, I couldn't believe it had happened again. That dog was outside.

I don't know how many garden fences I heaved it over that time, but it must have been a lot, because the dog never came back to our garden.

That afternoon, Les' brother David, and his wife Jill, turned up. Covered in bandages, my finger stuck straight out, and it throbbed like hell as I struggled to open the presents they'd brought.

"I'll have a Pernod," I said as Les came in, carrying the tea. She gave me one of her looks, but I took no notice. Without a drink, I couldn't keep pretending that I was feeling fine.

And besides, it was about time I was allowed to celebrate being an expectant Dad.

We had to wait six weeks after Christmas before Les

went back into hospital to have a test called an amniocentesis to find out if the baby was alright.

It wasn't just going into hospital that Les was scared about that time. If Mr. Steptoe found the baby was abnormal in any way, he was going to abort it straight away.

Before Les had the implant, we had signed a document giving him permission to do that. If anything was really wrong with our child, we wouldn't have wanted it to be born anyway.

"I've seen the baby," Les told me, when I arrived at Oldham General at visiting time. Mr. Steptoe had done a scan to see which way the baby was lying inside Les, and he had shown her the photograph afterwards.

"It looked like a picture of the moon to me," Les said. But I could tell she was excited all the same.

The trouble was that it was too early in Les's pregnancy to do the amniocentesis, so she had to hang about in hospital for a few weeks. I returned to Bristol to drive my lorry, and went up to see her every weekend.

Sharon was around at home, but she had a boy friend, so she was out a lot, which left me sitting by myself in front of the television. The set was on for company more than anything else, as I couldn't seem to concentrate on anything except what was happening to Les.

Having injections and operations didn't bother me. If only I could have gone through it all instead of Les. At least it would have felt as if I was doing something, instead of sitting every night on my own.

Les wouldn't admit that she was really nervous about the amniocentesis, but I knew she was. To this day, I'll never know how that girl ever went through so much to have a baby. She was still the sort who screamed her head off if I just larked about with a knitting needle, pretending it was a hospital syringe.

The house felt like a morgue when Les wasn't about. It echoed in the same way as our prefab had done after my mother had died.

I kept telling myself that we were going to have a family. All this would be worth it in the end. But it didn't make me feel much better at that time.

I didn't sleep well either when Les wasn't beside me. I kept waking up, imagining I could feel her there. In bed I had even started to pray that she would soon be home. Then one night the phone rang.

Les was sobbing her heart out on the other end.

"Mr. Steptoe tried to do the amniocentesis today, but he couldn't manage it. I was too worked up," she told me.

"Now I'm getting pains in my tummy. I'm sure I'm going to lose the baby."

Les was in a general ward at Oldham Hospital with women who were having miscarriages and abortions.

"One girl lost her baby today," Les said. "She was ever so upset, even though she's already got another child."

Les knew there was a slight risk that the amniocentesis might cause a miscarriage, though Mr. Steptoe had assured her that he had done the test dozens of times without a single miscarriage. But she'd got herself in a terrible state about it all the same.

"Keep your hair on," I told her. "I'm coming up."

How I was going to manage to stay in Oldham was another matter. I barely had enough money for the petrol to get me there. Staying in digs near the hospital each weekend had made me skint. But I had to see Les somehow.

"We're off to Oldham tomorrow," I told Sharon when she got in. Sharon was always moaning about being left with Les' brother when I went up there, so I put a sleeping bag for her into the car. Blankets, a primus stove, some tins of food, and even the dog Sheltie, who is a great big sheepdog, were piled in.

"You'll have to rough it," I warned Sharon. It was a long time since I'd slept in a car.

Les was in a totally different mood when we reached the hospital. "I've had it. I've had my amniocentesis," she cried, her face beaming. "And it didn't hurt at all."

Mr. Steptoe had tricked her into it. Les had felt so pleased when he told her that he wasn't going to do the amniocentesis for a few days. She was chatting to another girl when he came back unexpectedly.

"Come on, Lesley," he said. "It's time for your amniocentesis." She didn't even have time to get worked up again.

Les was settling down in her nice, warm bed as Sharon and I left. "Where are you staying tonight, Mr. Brown?" the hospital sister asked.

"The back of the car," I replied. "I left it too late to book into a hotel."

"Oh, you can't spend a night like that," the sister said, and gave me a phone number of a boarding house. I didn't like to mention that I couldn't afford anywhere else.

Sharon and I got some fish and chips from a Chinese restaurant and parked the car on some waste ground behind the hospital. The lights were off in the wards, as I brewed some coffee on the primus stove and settled Sharon in her sleeping bag.

"I must be mad," I thought to myself as I walked the dog across the waste ground. I was wearing a short-sleeved shirt, a pair of jeans and carpet slippers, and it was a freezing night.

Sharon was already asleep, as snug as a bug in her

sleeping bag, when I got back. I wrapped myself in a blanket, and turned one way and then the other. But there was no way I could get comfortable on those car seats.

When I was in Oldham, I usually stayed at Laura's place. Laura was an old girl knocking sixty, and quite a character she was too. Hot milk and whisky was her tipple and she got through six pints of milk a night. No one counted the bottles of whisky, but she must have knocked back quite a few on the quiet, as she was merry almost every night.

Those cotton sheets of Laura's were icy cold, and the bed creaked like hell, but it was a damned sight more comfortable than in the car. Sharon snored all night, and when I turned towards the dog, it licked me all over my face.

Frost coated the car windows when Sharon woke up next morning. Tinned minced beef and onions heated up on the primus stove was our breakfast.

Laura's guests would be tucking into their eggs and bacon. You could have as much as you could eat at Laura's place, and I was still starving after that minced beef.

"Come on," I told Sharon, stretching my stiffened limbs. "Let's tidy up the car."

Sharon looked as fresh as if she'd spent the night in a top-class hotel. Even the dog was enjoying itself, sniffing about the waste ground. How I was going to get through another night like that I didn't know. Sharon could have the dog next to her. It could lick her face all night.

Mr. Steptoe was examining Les when we arrived at the hospital. She was in a room on her own by that time, as Mr. Steptoe didn't like her being upset by what happened to the other patients in the big ward.

"Come in, Mr. Brown," Mr. Steptoe said. I still shook every time I saw him.

It was his abrupt manner that scared me, though he didn't mean anything by it. It was just his way of being businesslike. But he was a different man with Les. I always let her do the talking when Mr. Steptoe was around. He even called her Lesley. Those two got on like a house on fire.

"Put your ear to that," Mr. Steptoe told me, as he held an instrument on Les' tummy. She was grinning like a Cheshire cat.

Something was beating through the instrument. It was a fast beat, faster than the ticking of a clock.

"That's your baby's heart," Mr. Steptoe said. My chest swelled, but I didn't say much in front of him. When I got outside though, I couldn't stop telling Sharon about what I'd heard.

The blokes at work would be pleased as well. The foreman always wished me luck when I went to see Les. He knew how long we'd waited for a child, but he had no idea how it had come about.

Everything improved after seeing Les that morning. We didn't even have to spend another night in the car, as Les forked out the money I'd left her in hospital in case she needed anything.

"Wife alright?" Laura asked, when Sharon and I turned up. Laura had a good idea what was happening to Les, but she wasn't the sort to pry.

She also never let me down. Even if the digs were full up, Laura always put me up somehow.

Les finally came out of hospital, still not knowing the result of the amniocentesis. We had been told that we would have to wait another three weeks to find out if the baby was alright. As it got closer to the date, we watched for the postman every morning. We were both on such tenterhooks, we hardly slept at night.

It wasn't because Les had had the implant that it worried us. Having an abnormal child could happen to anyone who had had a normal pregnancy, and it was on our minds as much as any couple who had waited for so many years to have a baby.

"I don't feel anything's wrong," Les kept saying. But only the tests could tell that for sure. When the three weeks had passed without a letter from the hospital, we didn't know what to think any more.

"Oh, you poor thing," Dr. Hinton said, when Les went up to the fertility clinic and told her how worried she felt. She picked up the phone at once and spoke to Dr. Edwards at the hospital. As it turned out, Mr. Steptoe was away on holiday.

"I cried all the way home," Les told me, when she got back from the clinic. "Everyone in the street looked at me as if I was a nutcase, but I couldn't help myself. It was such a relief to know at last.

"Do you know what Dr. Hinton told me after she'd phoned the hospital?

"She said: 'Little baby Brown is perfectly alright.'"

Our Family Album

Christmas Day with Lesley (left), cousin Judith, and Gran's son Peter.

Lesley's Gran with Aunt Peggy and two of Peggy's children.

Lesley and her mother.

Lesley's mother with her stepsister Lorraine.

Lesley's brother David, Lesley, and two cousins, Judith and Andrea.

*Our wedding day. From left to right : Lesley's brother
David, John's daughter Sharon, John, Lesley, and Kate.*

OVERLEAF: *A few days before Louise's birth.*

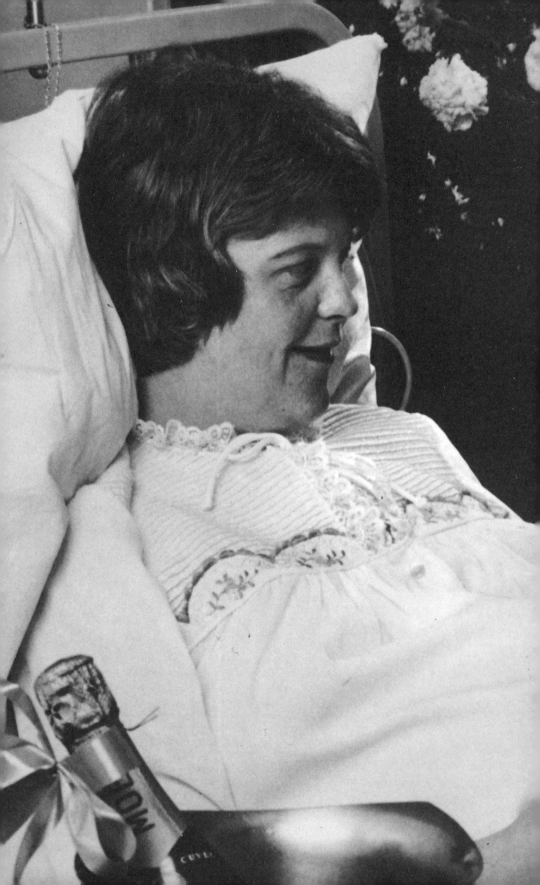

Louise's birth certificate.

No fee is chargeable for this certificate

GG 705097

1 & 2 ELIZ. 2 CH. 20

CERTIFICATE
OF BIRTH

Name and Surname Louise Joy BROWN

Sex Female

Date of Birth Twenty Fifth July 1978

Place of Birth {
Registration District Oldham
Sub-district Boundary Park
}

I, JOAN BAMFORD Registrar of Births and Deaths
for the sub-district of BOUNDARY PARK in the
Registration District of OLDHAM do hereby
certify that the above particulars have been compiled from an entry in
a register in my custody.

Date — 3 AUG 1978

Joan Bamford
Registrar of Births and Deaths.

YPAOT 25

CAUTION:—Any person who (1) falsifies any of the particulars on this certificate, or
(2) uses a falsified certificate as true, knowing it to be false, is liable to prosecution.

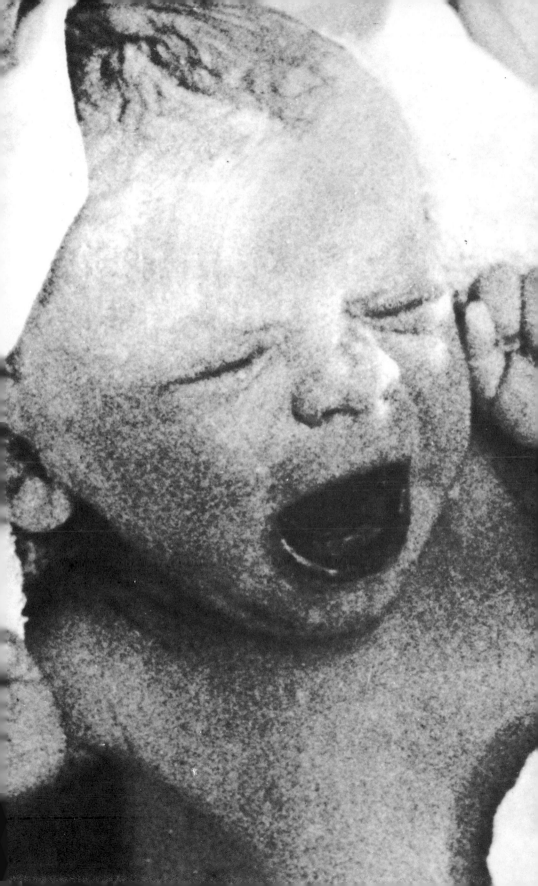

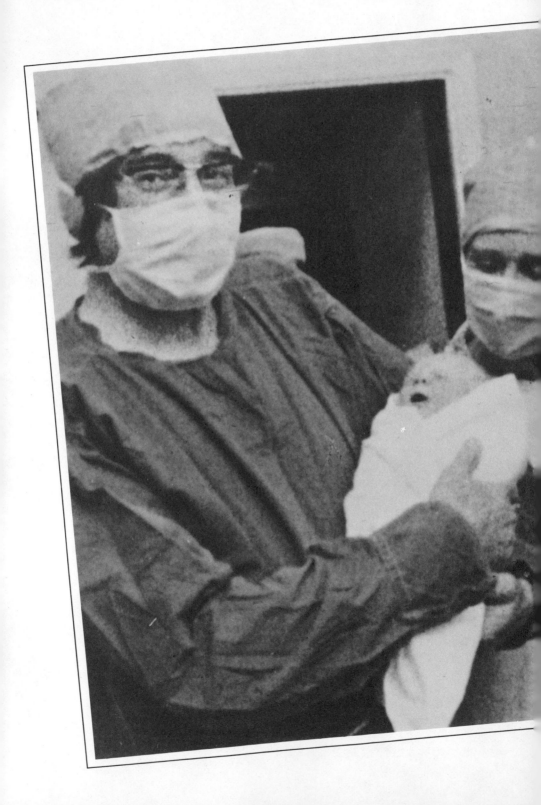

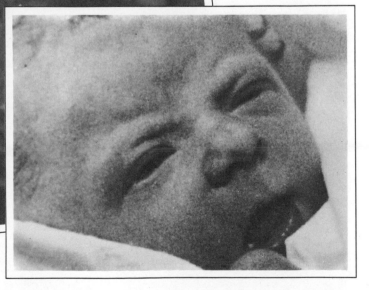

Dr. Edwards holds Louise in the operating theatre. Mr. Steptoe and Dr. Edwards' assistant, Jean Purdy, are also present.
KEYSTONE PRESS AGENCY LTD.

OVERLEAF:
Our miracle, at last.
ASSOCIATED NEWSPAPERS GROUP LTD.

Louise opens her eyes.
KEYSTONE PRESS AGENCY LTD.

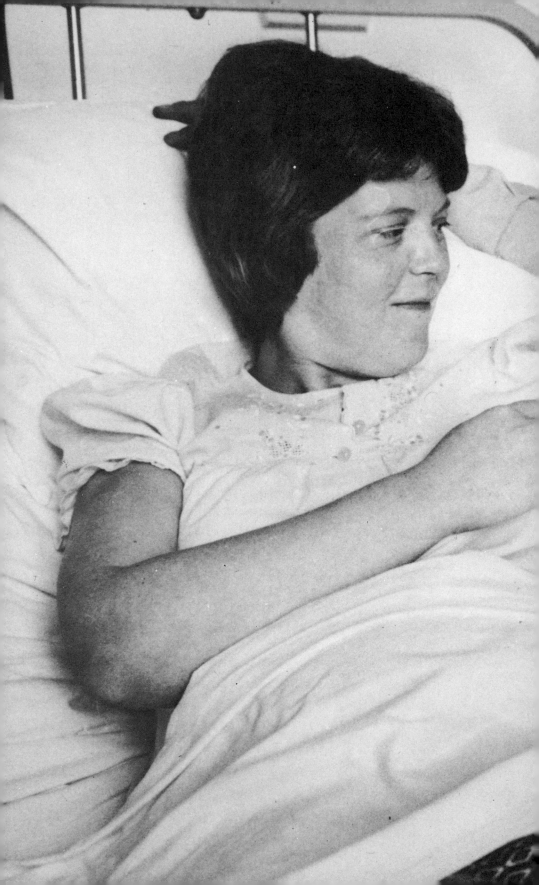

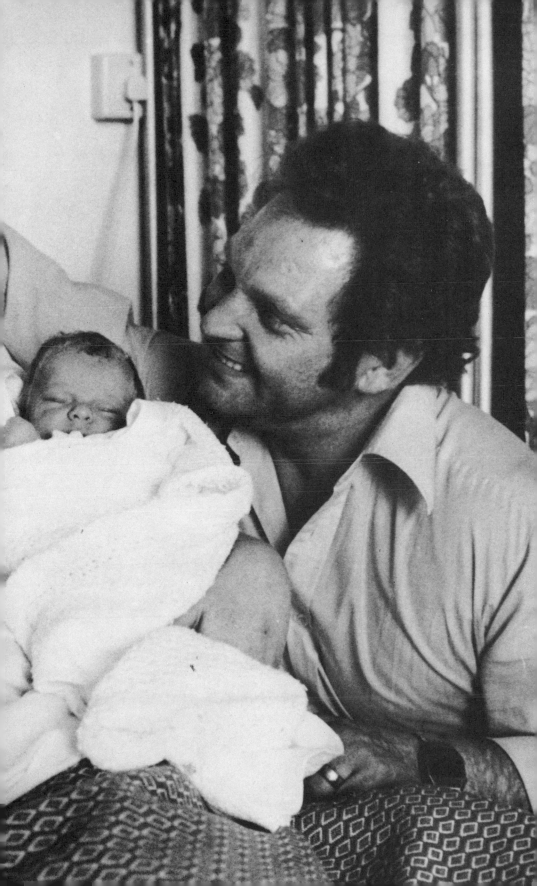

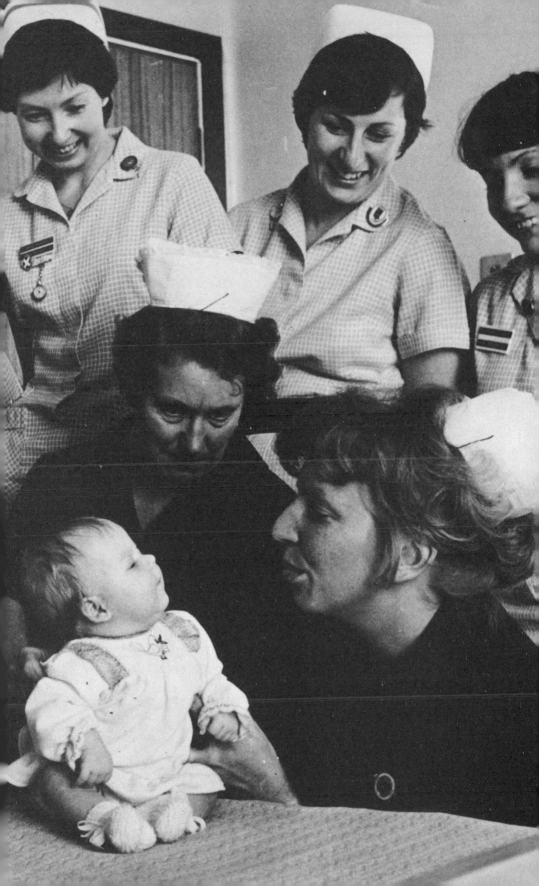

Lesley and Louise, with some of the thousands of cards bringing congratulations from all over the world.

PREVIOUS PAGES:
Three-month-old Louise performing for nurses at Oldham General.
ASSOCIATED NEWSPAPERS GROUP LTD.

Out with baby Louise and our dog Sheltie.

OPPOSITE: *Gran, shortly before her death, with great granddaughter Louise.*

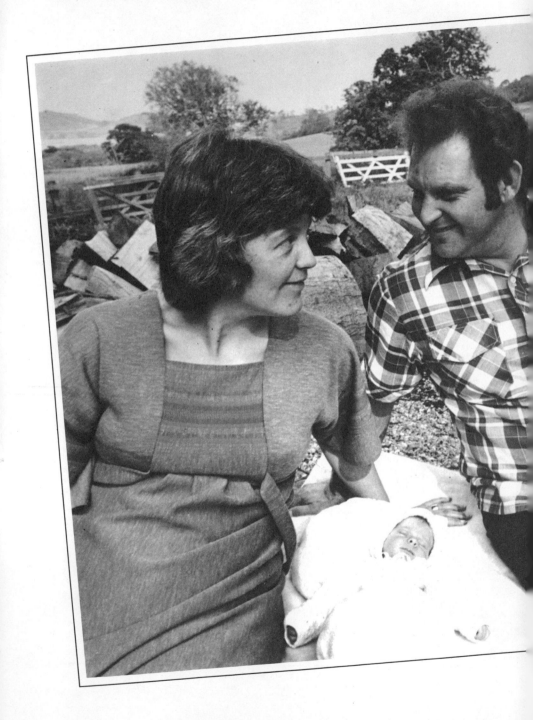

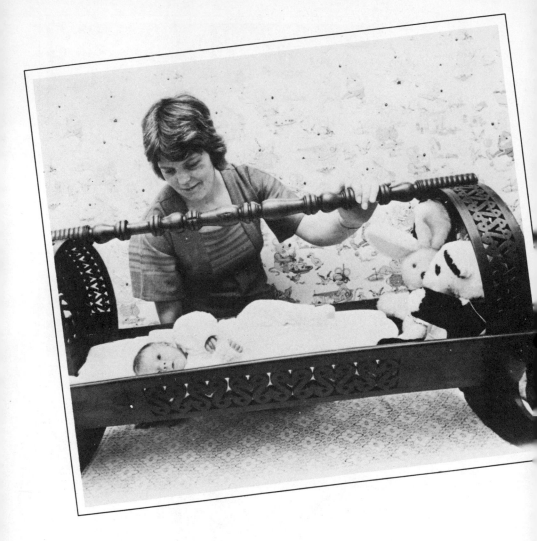

In the nursery with Louise. The cradle was a gift from the people of Turkey.
ASSOCIATED NEWSPAPERS GROUP LTD.

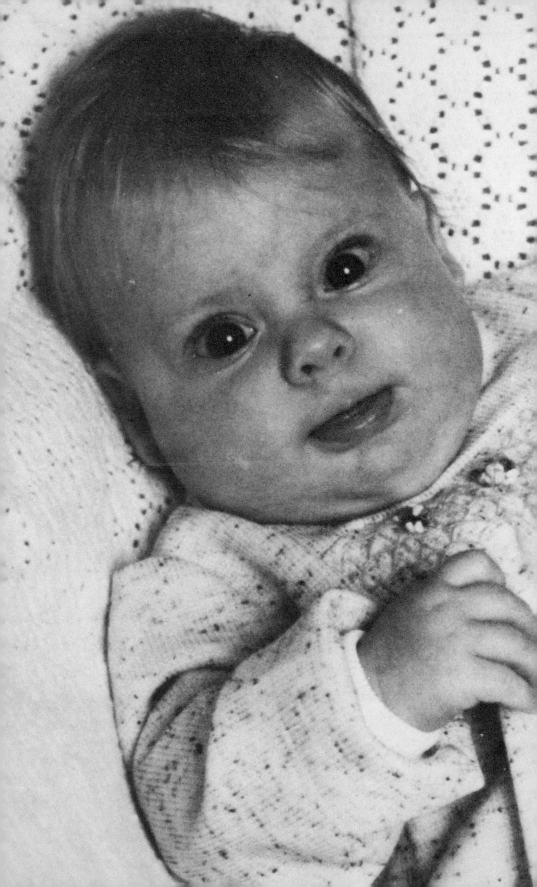

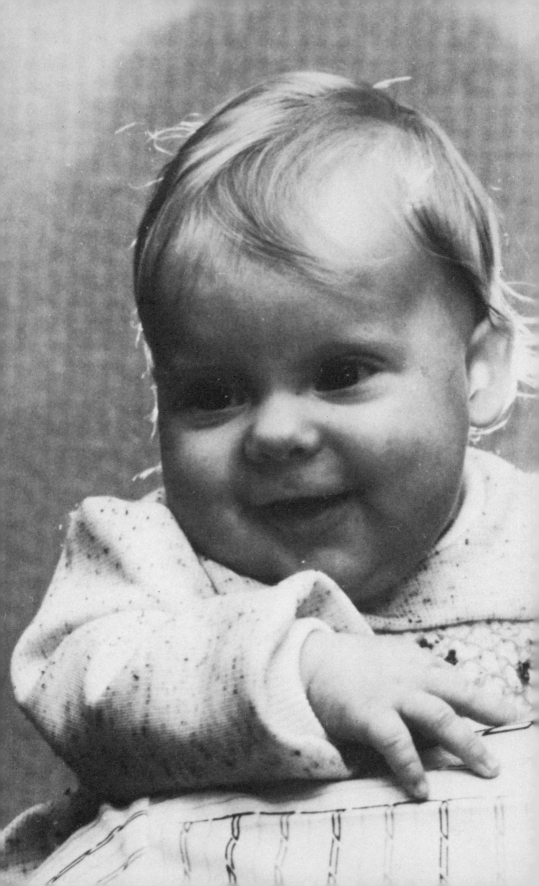

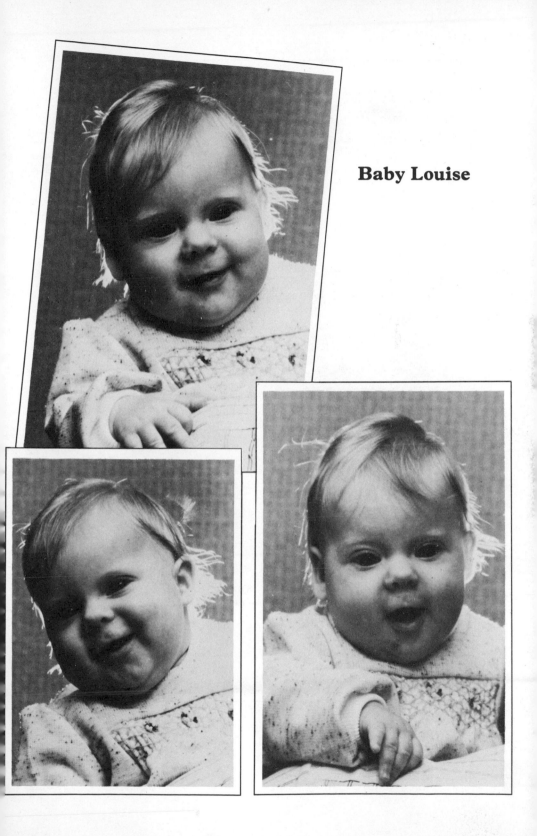

Baby Louise

Our new family.

Sharon with Louise.

CHAPTER FOURTEEN

*Lesley suddenly realises how special her
baby's going to be.*

M R. STEPTOE PUT HIS arms around me: "You're
going to do it for us, aren't you, Lesley?" I
was six months' pregnant, and even knitting
for the baby. So I was sure I was going to do it.

Mr. Steptoe took such good care of me. He wasn't
going to let anything go wrong.

Already I was known in the hospital as Mr. Steptoe's favourite, because he came to see me every day. It
must have seemed odd to the other patients, as they had
no idea about the implant.

So secret had it all become that I wasn't even
allowed to use my proper name. I had been booked into
the hospital as Rita Ferguson, and Mr. Steptoe had
made up an address for me in Oldham, which I had
learnt by heart.

After he'd hugged me, Mr. Steptoe's expression
changed.

"I'm sorry, Lesley," he said. "I'm afraid I can't let
you go home tomorrow." I had been in Oldham Hospital having tests for a fortnight, and I had been counting
the days.

I had got myself so excited about being home with John again that, when Mr. Steptoe said I couldn't go, I burst into tears.

"As long as you remember you're Rita Ferguson, you can mix with the other patients," Mr. Steptoe had told me when he gave me the false name. But I was too scared I might be caught out, so I never did. And it was so lonely there all day on my own.

My room was near the labour ward and, at night, I lay awake for hours listening to the screams of women having their babies. I kept imagining what it would be like when it came to my turn.

"You promised I could go home tomorrow," I told Mr. Steptoe. He had never broken his word to me before.

"Have you seen the morning papers?" he asked. I shook my head.

"There's a lot about you in the local paper," he went on. "Luckily they don't know who you are. It just says you're an Oldham woman."

What he said didn't really hit me at the time. With all the secrecy that went on about me, I wasn't surprised that no one had found out about those hundreds of women I still imagined had had their babies from implants. But compared with all the big things that went on in the world, what had happened to me didn't seem much to make a fuss about. Fancy that local paper being interested in me, I thought.

What was much more on my mind was all I had to do at home to get ready for the baby. John had wanted to rush out and buy baby things as soon as we knew the implant had worked. But it was too early to push our luck. I was sure something would go wrong if we did that.

But now that I was well and truly pregnant, it was a different matter. John had bought a second-hand cot for

£10 off a bloke at work. It looked almost brand new. Whenever I had a bit of money to spare, I went round baby shops buying vests, baby gowns and the smallest-sized rubber pants.

How we were going to find the money for a pram worried me a lot. It had never occurred to us before that we couldn't really afford to have a child. In all those years of wanting one, it had been the last thing to cross our minds.

Mr. Steptoe watched as I got myself into a right old state. "Alright," he said. "But you'll go home straight away, before the newspapers have a chance to find out who you are."

I stopped crying at once. Now I was even going a day earlier than I'd thought.

"I'm not having you travelling alone," Mr. Steptoe carried on. "My wife will go with you on the train."

Mr. Steptoe had brought his wife into the hospital to meet me, so I knew she wasn't young. I wasn't going to have her put out like that. Mr. Steptoe didn't usually make such a fuss.

His wife put me on the train at Manchester instead. She was a real lady, but not a bit stuck-up. She treated me that day as if I was as precious as gold.

"Thank you ever so much," I said, as she settled me in a carriage with some magazines to read.

Mrs. Steptoe seemed nervous. She kept looking over her shoulder, as if someone might be following us.

"Are you sure you'll be alright?" she asked for the umpteenth time.

I felt absolutely fine. "Oh yes, it's a straight through train, and John will be at Bristol to meet me," I assured her.

Mr. Steptoe had insisted before I left that John should be waiting for me. So I rang my cousin Judith to give him a message, as John wasn't expecting me until the following day.

Mrs. Steptoe stood on the platform. I couldn't think of anything else to say. "There's no need for you to wait," I told her. But she wouldn't leave until the train pulled out.

"Go carefully, my dear. Hold on tight," said people in the train corridor, as I made my way to the buffet. My big tummy bulged under a maternity smock, and I thought how lovely it looked. Everyone seemed so glad for me.

It had been the same when I told the women in the cheese factory, when I went back to pack in my job. They thought I'd had an operation that had unblocked my Fallopian tubes, and they were so pleased that it had worked. As I chatted to them in the canteen about being pregnant, I remembered how envious I'd once felt of other girls who had come in with the same news.

I bought a cup of coffee and a few bars of chocolate from the train buffet. "Watch it," said the woman behind the counter, as the train lurched. "I don't want to be a midwife on this journey."

I smiled at her. "There's someone a lot more special than you who is going to see my baby is born alright," I thought to myself.

Suddenly I began to understand why such an important doctor as Mr. Steptoe was so anxious about me. I thought back to the way he talked about that newspaper finding out about my baby.

"Mr. Steptoe has never had a success before," the nurses had warned me after the implant. Perhaps there weren't hundreds of babies like mine. There must be just a few, I told myself. I still couldn't believe that mine was really the first.

As the train sped towards Bristol, I thought about

what my baby would be like. "This is going to be a very special baby. Not just special to John and me," I said to myself.

A few people waited on the platform at Bristol Temple Meads Station, but John was nowhere to be seen. He couldn't have got my message. But that didn't matter, since we lived quite near the station. Whatever Mr. Steptoe thought, I could easily get home on my own.

There was a queue for taxis, but I was too impatient to wait. After being away for a fortnight, I was so anxious to get back home. If I walked, John would probably bump into me on the way.

My two suitcases weren't heavy. They just had my night things and knitting for the baby inside. But the trouble was that I was such a size. Soon I was too out of breath to go any further. I struggled to the Rediffusion shop, where my sister-in-law Jill worked.

Jill spotted me through the plate glass window. "What on earth are you doing here today?" she asked, rushing out.

"Mr. Steptoe wanted me out of the way. The newspapers got hold of something about my being pregnant," I said.

"Well there's nothing very unusual in that," Jill replied. Even though we had explained to the family exactly how I got pregnant, none of them had really been able to take it in.

I wouldn't let Jill take me home. John might be there, and I wanted to surprise him on my own. I just left my suitcases with Jill.

His car was parked outside the house, so I knocked on the front door. John's mouth dropped open when he saw me standing there. Judith hadn't been able to reach him to tell him I was on my way.

"Our baby's going to be very special," I said, and then burst into tears. I got upset so easily when I was pregnant. I cried at the slightest thing.

"And you're special too," said John. "So you're going straight up to bed. Why you do daft things like walking from the station, I don't know. You never listen to advice from anyone, not even Mr. Steptoe."

"Oh yes, I do," I said.

I told John about the newspaper in Oldham being interested in us. "I don't think many babies can have been born like ours," I said.

"You could be right," John replied.

Next morning, John rushed home from work in a real rage. "We're all over the front of the bloody newspapers," he cried. I was sitting on the sofa in my dressing gown, knitting a cardigan for the baby at the time.

"Test Tube Baby by the Summer," read one headline. "A Miracle Birth," said another.

The newspapers still didn't know my name. They also hadn't found out that Mr. Steptoe had made up my address. I was still supposed to come from Oldham.

The reports said the baby was expected in July. Those reporters didn't know the exact date, but for that matter, neither did I. Mr. Steptoe hadn't even told me that.

The papers said my baby was going to be a miracle —the first one. I burst into tears all over again.

"Don't get in a state," said John, when suddenly there was a loud knock at the door. We looked at each other. It was probably only the milkman. After all, those newspapers had no idea I lived in Bristol.

"I'm from the *Sun* newspaper," the man outside the door told John. "Are you the father of the test tube child?"

There were those words again. Mr. Steptoe had

never referred to my baby like that. How dare anyone call it a test tube child.

John glanced back at me, and then went outside with the newspaper reporter, shutting the door after him. The next thing I knew, he was tapping on the back window and beckoning to me.

"Get your clothes on," John told me, as I opened the window, still in my dressing gown. "We've got to get out of here before that journalist realises that there's a back door to this house."

Of course I went all to pieces. I don't know what clothes I managed to pull on. It seemed so awful being driven out of my own home, especially when I had so much to get ready for the baby.

Since I'd been pregnant, John hadn't allowed me in his lorry, in case I got bumped about. But now there was no other choice. He bundled me up beside him and drove off, leaving the journalist still waiting outside the front door.

We went round to my brother's house to ask if we could stay there with him and Jill until all the fuss had died down.

"Why should newspaper reporters be chasing you?" David asked, as if we'd gone completely mad. "You said hundreds of women had had babies like yours."

"I made a mistake," I said. "I'm the first one."

CHAPTER FIFTEEN

John gets his miracle.

"T HIS WILL BE A very important baby—not just to you and Lesley, but to the rest of the world," Mr. Steptoe told me.

We were in the bar of a posh restaurant in Oldham, where Mr. Steptoe had asked me to meet him. When he'd phoned, I'd rushed up from Bristol at once. Les was in hospital, waiting for the birth, and, since Mr. Steptoe wanted to see me on my own, I wondered what was up.

He was in his usual dark suit, and I felt a bit uncomfortable standing beside him at the bar in an open-necked shirt. Then Dr. Edwards bounced in, raising a few eyebrows from that toffed-up crowd, as he was wearing a pair of scruffy trousers and an old T-shirt. But I felt better at once. You'd never guess Dr. Edwards was such an important doctor, as he was such a natural bloke.

"There's a lot of money involved over this birth," Mr. Steptoe told me, as he ordered another round of drinks. "Newspapers are already offering contracts to buy your story."

"How much are they offering?" I asked. I wondered

what he meant by a lot. "Would we get as much as £500?"

Mr. Steptoe laughed out loud. "I've a letter from an American newspaper in my briefcase offering you a contract worth something like a quarter of a million pounds," he said.

A chap at the other end of the bar choked on his beer.

Being an ordinary working-class bloke, I count money in tenners, not hundreds or thousands of pounds. A quarter of a million went straight over the top of my head.

"But I don't advise you to accept that offer," Mr. Steptoe told me. Well, that was a relief. Mr. Steptoe thought it would be better to accept a contract from a British newspaper instead.

"That's fine by me," I replied. "I'm a bit patriotic anyway."

"There's no way this can be a quiet birth," Mr. Steptoe continued. "Too much has been in the newspapers already."

"When it happens, every paper in the world will want the story, as there has never been a child born from an implant before.

"You do realise that your baby is the first?"

"That's just about dawned on us," I replied. It was a good job we hadn't known earlier, as Les would have gone to pieces and lost the baby if she had realised there was going to be such a hullabaloo.

"You must have nothing but the best for this baby," Mr Steptoe told me. "And the only way you can protect it from all the publicity is with money."

He explained that signing a contract with one newspaper meant we wouldn't have to talk to all the rest. We would control the publicity, and it would stop reporters from other papers hounding us so much. I had already had a taste of what that was like.

Les and I hadn't been able to go home for over a month since that reporter from the *Sun* had turned up at our front door. Once the newspapers had found out we were the parents of the "test tube" baby, journalists hung about outside our house all the time.

Mr. Steptoe got Les out of the way by taking her to his daughter's home in the country, and later she joined me at Dave and Jill's house. We managed to sneak home for a week, so Les could get the baby's things ready before she went back into hospital to wait for the birth. The press had given up watching the house by that time, as it had been empty for so long.

Mr. Steptoe opened his briefcase at the bar. Inside he had five contracts from British newspapers which were being offered to Les and me. One newspaper said it would top any offer made to us, but it was a sleazy rag, and I wanted a paper that would treat us with a bit of dignity.

Mr. Steptoe and Dr. Edwards seemed keen on the *Daily Mail*, and I thought that paper would do a fair job.

"How much do you think they'll give us?" I asked.

"Around £20,000," Mr. Steptoe replied.

As it turned out, the *Mail* gave us quite a bit more than that, though nothing like those fantastic sums other newspapers claimed we'd had. I've yet to see what a hundred thousand pounds looks like.

Twenty thousand didn't scare me as much as a quarter of a million had, but it still sounded a lot. I had never imagined even counting that sort of money, let alone being given it.

"What did Mr. Steptoe want?" Dave asked, when I got back to Bristol. My head still swam with all the talk about contracts for books, films and television that Mr.

Steptoe said we'd get after the baby arrived.

"Les and I are going to be worth a lot of money, by the sound of it," I told Dave. It didn't make any sense at all, when all we had wanted out of this was a child.

There was a security guard outside Les' room, and several others guarded the doors and corridors all over Oldham General Hospital to stop journalists getting to her.

There was no knowing what lengths those reporters, who waited all day in the hospital grounds, would go to for a story. A couple of them had already dressed up as nuns, with a press bloke pretending to be a priest, and asked if they could give comfort to my wife. An American reporter started a bomb scare, hoping to catch Les as the expectant mothers were evacuated from the maternity wing. When the police discovered who he was, he was booted out of Oldham fast.

I sneaked into the hospital by a back door at the crack of dawn, so as not to be spotted by the press. One security officer had been offered £5,000 to tip off a newspaper about which door I used, but I don't think he ever did.

"Morning," I said to the security man outside Les' door. He was called Geoff and we got to know him quite well through all this.

Les' room was like a blooming florist's shop. Flowers from newspapers and magazines arrived each day, with messages asking Les to talk to them. The nurses always removed these messages before giving her the bouquets.

That day there was the most enormous basket of flowers I'd ever seen standing beside her bed. It must have cost more than a hundred pounds.

"I've been so upset about those flowers," Les said. "I've hardly slept all night because the nurses wouldn't tell me who sent them. I got worked up not knowing who they were from."

Mr. Steptoe had told her in the end. It was another lot from the *Daily Express*.

It didn't take much to upset Les, as she'd been stuck for over a month in the same hospital room. The only time she was allowed outside was when she was taken to be weighed, and then screens were put up at either end of the corridor so no one could get a glimpse of her.

Even the window in her room was out of bounds. She couldn't go near it as television and newspaper cameras were trained on it, waiting to get a shot of her. The nurses had put up net curtains, but even those didn't help. Those newspaper photographers had telescopic lenses which could penetrate the net.

Even I felt as if I was in a cage in Les' room, and I didn't have to stay there all the time. It was no wonder Les got so depressed.

"I'm not even allowed to watch certain programmes on the television, in case I'm upset by something that's being said about me," Les went on. "Last night, I was just about to watch 'What the Papers Say', when the night nurse came in and switched the set off."

The hospital staff often wouldn't let her see the newspapers now that so much was in them about us.

"That's ridiculous," I exploded. "You'll have to face the publicity when you get out of here. It's best if you start getting used to it now."

Les glanced towards the window. More than twenty reporters and photographers waited below. "I don't think I'll ever get used to it," she said.

Mr. Steptoe had hoped Les could go home again before the baby was born, but that was impossible now that all those journalists were after her. If only we knew how much longer we had to wait. But Mr. Steptoe wasn't sure of that himself. The baby might not be born until August, and we weren't halfway through July yet.

How Les was going to get through it, cooped up in that room, I didn't like to think.

"Mr. Steptoe's worried that the baby's so small," Les said.

I was put in a shoe box lined with cotton wool when I was born, since I only weighed 1 pound 4 ounces. Being tiny hadn't done me any harm. All Brown babies are usually small.

"Don't worry about that," I told Les. "That baby of ours obviously takes after its Dad."

Paul Vincent, Mr. Steptoe's solicitor, arrived with the *Daily Mail* contract for Les and me to sign. I was only too anxious to get the protection of a newspaper that Mr. Steptoe had talked about. In many ways, I was just as much a prisoner as Les. I was hiding from the press under the name of Ron Ferguson in an Oldham hotel. After seeing Les, I went straight back to my hotel room. I never even dared to go out for a pint.

"The *Mail* will be sending some reporters to interview you," Paul Vincent told Les. "There will be photographers too."

She didn't look at all keen. "It's better than having that lot down there forever chasing us," I said.

"Oh, I don't know what's best," Les replied. "I just want to be left alone to have my baby." She signed the contract all the same.

"We can afford to buy the pram now," I told her. Les had been so worried about not having the money to get a pram before.

"I'd like an armchair for the baby's room as well, so I can sit in there at feeding times," Les said.

"I expect we can afford that now," I replied.

A security officer had a list of all the car registration numbers belonging to the reporters who were outside the hospital. There were about a hundred in all and, before I left, he checked through the list, to make sure none was parked near mine.

The coast seemed clear, but I put on a pair of dark glasses, just in case. You never could tell if those journalists had spotted you until it was too late.

Just when I thought I'd got away with it, six reporters' cars appeared from nowhere and chased mine out of the hospital gates. I put my foot down and lost five of them, but a little blue sports car still stuck to me like a leech.

It felt like I was in a film. It was real cops and robbers stuff.

I remembered all those months back, when I was wondering if it was worth going through so much to have a baby. I hadn't even known the half of it then.

Looking in my driving mirror, I recognised the face of the reporter who was driving the blue sports car. He hadn't realised it, but that press bloke had been drinking in the same pub as me the night before. I had got so cheesed off just going back to the hotel that, after seeing Les, I took a chance and had a quick one at the Running Horse just across the road from the hospital.

The landlord started chatting and, noticing my accent, asked where I was from. I had to be careful over that one.

"Down South," I told him. "I'm subcontracted at the hospital to rebuild the laundry that caught fire."

"Heard anything about the baby?" the landlord asked.

"What baby?" My face was a picture of innocence.

"There's a test tube baby being born in that hospital," he told me.

"Go on," I replied.

"There are swarms of newspaper reporters up here to get the story," the landlord continued. "There's a couple over there now."

He pointed to two blokes having a pint. The one who was now chasing me in his sports car glanced at me and then went back to his beer.

"Those pressmen get on my bleeding nerves," the landlord said. "They harass my customers about whether they know the father of the baby all the time."

"Still, I can't complain in one way," he went on. "Every time those reporters buy a drink, they stuff a cigar in my pocket. I get a good price selling their cigars when they've gone."

How that reporter would kick himself if he found the chance he'd missed. As his car and mine pulled up at traffic lights, I couldn't resist taking off my dark glasses and giving him a big grin.

His expression was a picture, as he realised that he'd seen me in that pub the night before. Before he recovered from the shock, I shot off again. But it took over four hours of hard driving to get that blue sports car off my tail.

Tuesday, July 25th, arrived, and I turned up later at the hospital than I usually did. Now that the *Daily Mail* had sent reporters to look after me, I didn't have to sneak in at dawn. The *Mail* used nine different cars as decoys, so the journalists outside the hospital got confused. To make it even more difficult to spot me, I had to lie down in the back of the car as we shot through the hospital gates.

As soon as I saw Les that morning, I knew something was wrong. She had gone really quiet.

"What's up?" I asked.

"Nothing."

"Out with it, missus. You can't fool me."

"I'm going to have the baby tonight," she whispered. "But Mr. Steptoe said I wasn't even to tell you."

You could have knocked me down with a feather.
We had thought the birth wouldn't be for another couple
of weeks.

The baby was to be born by Caesarian section,
which meant an operation. But Les didn't even seem to
mind the thought of that. She was so calm, whereas I
was shaking like a leaf.

"I had to tell you," Les said. "You're the father.
You've a right to know."

When Mr. Steptoe came in, we both looked guilty.
"Can I have a word, John?" he asked.

"Don't let on," Les whispered, as I followed him
outside. I was better with him now that he called me by
my first name.

"Owing to Lesley's condition, we're going to deliver the baby tonight," he told me, pacing up and down
the corridor. "I'm a little concerned that the child isn't
putting on weight."

I pretended to be flabbergasted all over again.

"Don't worry," he said, still pacing about. "Everything will be alright."

It was arranged that I would leave the hospital at
my usual time and wait for a phone call that night so I
could get back in time for the birth.

"What's up?" asked Dave Norris, one of the *Daily
Mail* reporters who was staying with me. Since I'd got
back from the hospital, I had started pacing the floor,
just like Mr. Steptoe.

The house I was staying in was owned by the
mother of one of the *Daily Mail* photographers. It was
in one of the posher parts of Oldham. Sharon was there,

as well as a neighbour of ours from Bristol, called Margaret, who had come to keep Sharon company while I was at the hospital with Les.

"Les wasn't herself today," I told Dave. "I'm sure something's wrong."

Those *Mail* reporters who stayed with me were a nice bunch of chaps, and I should really have let them know what was going on. But there would have been such a commotion, with endless phone calls to their newspaper, more reporters and photographers arriving to ask me questions and take pictures all the time. I just didn't feel like all that fuss.

"Phone the hospital and see how she is," Dave suggested.

"No, I won't bother," I replied, still walking up and down.

Dave offered me a drink, but I shook my head. I'd been hitting the bottle far too much in the last few weeks. I usually had a few pints on the way home from the hospital, just to unwind, and then a few more when I got back to the house. Les got so depressed when I left the hospital. Unless I had a few, I couldn't get her off my mind.

But I'd vowed that I'd drink in moderation when the baby arrived.

As it turned out, that night Sharon was supposed to ring her boy friend, who would be waiting in a phone box between 10.45 and 11 o'clock for her call, the very time the hospital was due to ring. She was so excited about speaking to him. But I had to stop her using the phone somehow.

I beckoned to Margaret. "Come into the garden," I whispered. Dave didn't take any notice. It was a warm night, so we could have just been getting a breath of air.

"Do it how you like, but you've got to keep Sharon

off that phone," I told Margaret. "I'm taking you into my confidence.

"Les is having the baby tonight."

Margaret started bawling. "Shut up, you daft woman." Dave would guess at once if he heard her carrying on like that.

She took Sharon off to get some fish and chips. It was a long walk to the fish shop, and they weren't back by eleven o'clock. By half past, though, I was pacing the floor again. The phone still hadn't rung.

"For goodness sake, call the hospital. You're making me nervous walking up and down all the time," Dave said. He was a nervous enough bloke already. A packet of cigarettes lasted Dave twenty minutes. Chain smoking as he did, his fingers had turned the colour of bark.

Edith, the nursing officer at the hospital, came on the line. "You'd better come over. Be careful," she said, and put down the phone.

I went on speaking to the dialling tone. "I'm a bit concerned about Les," I said as Dave was listening. "Alright, I'll come up."

"She's very restless tonight," I told Dave, as I put the phone down. So he agreed to drive me to the hospital. We used a car that had been kept for emergencies and wasn't known by the rest of the press. Now that the birth was expected at any time, reporters hung about the hospital all night as well.

Dave wanted to wait for me. "There's no point," I said. "For all I know, I'll be there all night."

It wasn't nice having to lie to him. But Les and I had waited for this moment for so long, and I wanted us to share it on our own, like any normal couple.

"Alright," he agreed finally. "I won't wait. But don't forget to phone."

The lights were out in Les' room, so there was no

hint to the reporters outside of what was going on.

Les and I sat in the darkness, not saying much. She was dressed in a white operating gown. I still couldn't get over how calm she was.

"It won't be long now before you see the baby," she said, and I squeezed her hand. I was still shaking all over.

The trolley arrived to take her to the operating theatre, and Les waved as the nurse wheeled her out of the room. "Bye, bye," she said.

Mrs. Steptoe appeared. "Come on, John. Let's have a cup of tea."

There was a programme about golf on in the television room. I tried to think of something to say to Mrs. Steptoe about the game, but my mind was elsewhere. I kept trying to imagine what was happening to Les.

Mrs. Steptoe started cracking jokes. She told me about all the trouble she'd had over her name, after the television programme "Steptoe and Son" about the rag-and-bone men. Every time she went to a restaurant, they asked if she'd left her horse and cart outside.

She was trying hard, but I still felt as if Mrs. Steptoe and I had been in the television room for days. Then a sister knocked at the door.

"There's a security guard coming to take you to the operating theatre, Mr. Brown," she said.

Screens covered all the doors that led to the theatre. Dozens of policemen and security officers lined every corridor as I walked along. It felt as if I was moving in a dream.

Dr. Edwards rushed forward as I walked through the double doors into the reception area. "Congratulations," he cried, shaking my hand. Inside the operating theatre, a baby was screaming its head off.

Mr. Steptoe was putting a little baby into an incubator as Dr. Edwards led me inside.

"Here you are, John," Mr. Steptoe said. "Here's your daughter."

"Don't film Mr. Brown, please," he yelled at the film crew who had filmed the birth, as I burst into tears.

Edith, the nursing officer, a security guard and three policemen squeezed into a lift with me, to go up to the premature unit where the baby was taken as a precaution, in case the press managed to get through the hospital's security screen.

Edith put a white gown on me. Then she lifted the baby out of the incubator and into my arms. I could hardly hold her, I was still shaking so much.

She started to cry again. That baby of ours had the loudest yell. When she started, she woke up all the other babies in the maternity block.

Edith took her from me and put her in a little cot. I just wanted to sit there and look at my daughter. She was a miracle, just because Les and I had waited so long for her.

Finally Edith shooed me away. I went back to see Les. But, after having an anaesthetic for the operation, she was still out for the count.

It was about time I kept my word to the *Daily Mail*.

"Hello, Dave," I said, as a sleepy voice answered the phone.

"Just letting you know it's a girl. Five pounds, twelve ounces."

And with that, I put down the phone.

CHAPTER SIXTEEN

Lesley takes Louise home.

"LESLEY, LESLEY," SOMEONE was shaking me awake.
"Do you want to see your baby?"
The anaesthetic had hardly started to wear off. My eyelids felt like lead as I tried to open them.

Through a haze, I saw the outline of a little baby being held in front of me. "It's a girl," a voice said. Then I must have fallen straight back to sleep again.

"Who loves you, baby?" Mr. Steptoe had asked me, earlier that day, when he came into my room. He had been down to watch a scan being taken of the baby, which he never usually did. When we got inside my room again, he seemed so excited I had guessed something was up.

He didn't tell me until later that the baby was probably going to be born that night.

"Don't tell anyone, not even John," he said. "It's not definite yet."

But, just in case, I wasn't allowed to eat any supper. "Don't leave anything on your plate," Mr. Steptoe warned me. "Get rid of the food somehow. Otherwise the nurses will suspect something's going on."

If Mr. Steptoe had had his way, no one would have been any the wiser about me until after the baby was born. He had done his best to keep it quiet, so that all those journalists wouldn't be waiting outside the hospital all the time.

As well as having a false name and address, my hospital records were also forgeries. Mr. Steptoe kept all his notes about me in his pocket diary.

But someone on the hospital staff had found out and told the press. Now we had to be so careful that even the woman who cleaned my room had been replaced when she started asking me too many questions.

Information still leaked out. Newspaper headlines like "Test Tube Baby Almost Dies" and "Crisis over Miracle Child" were exaggerated, but they still appeared at times when I had minor problems like toxaemia and a hormone deficiency.

That evening, Mr. Steptoe's wife arrived just before my supper was due. She popped in almost every day to cheer me up, and she often brought little treats to eat as well.

Usually it was a prawn cocktail, but that time it was raspberries and a pot of cream. I was trying to think of an excuse not to eat them, when the nurse walked in with my supper.

"That lettuce leaf is dirty," Mrs. Steptoe complained, as I looked at the soup, salad and pink blancmange on my tray. She was always worried about me having decent food.

"I'm sorry, Mrs. Steptoe, but I can't even eat your raspberries," I said. "Mr. Steptoe thinks the baby might be born tonight."

She wouldn't tell anyone. After all, she was his wife.

"I'm not supposed to be telling you," I added, just in case.

Mrs. Steptoe looked excited too. "How are we going to get rid of all this food?" she giggled.

The soup went down the wash basin. We packed the salad and blancmange in plastic bags, and Mrs. Steptoe disappeared with them in her handbag.

"You have eaten well tonight," commented the nurse, as she collected my empty tray.

At ten o'clock, the lights went out as usual in my room, so the reporters in the grounds below imagined I was settling down for another night.

By torchlight, Edna, the nursing officer, and a hospital sister, got me ready for the operation. It was quite a job, fixing up all the paraphernalia almost in the dark.

John came in when they had finished. I had told him, too, before I was supposed to have done. Well, he was the baby's father. It wasn't a secret I could have kept from him.

As we sat together in the darkness, I thought how different our lives would be in just a little while.

Since I'd known the baby was alright, I hadn't really worried any more. I had known that we would end up with a child.

There had been a moment when I thought I'd ruined it all. Just before I'd come back into hospital, I'd fallen down the stairs at home. But, as Mr. Steptoe said, on those occasions it's usually the mother, not the baby, who gets hurt and, sure enough, I'd ached for days.

Nothing would go wrong now because I was in Mr. Steptoe's hands. He was going to deliver a perfect baby.

"I'm glad all the waiting's over," I told John. "You'll see the baby in a little while."

John squeezed my hand. I felt so calm, but his hand was shaking in mine.

"Bye, bye," I waved to him, as I was wheeled away

to the operating theatre. When I saw John again, it would be with the baby.

The anaesthetist put a mask over my face. "Breathe deeply," he said, and I gulped down the gas. I couldn't wait to get this operation over with.

"Lesley, do you want to see your baby?"

I had done it at last.

"Would you like to have your little girl?" Mr. Steptoe was with me the morning after she had been born, and he handed the baby to me, wrapped up in a shawl. Only her little face was peeping out. My first thought was how much she looked like John.

Mr. Steptoe stood watching me. "Thank you for my baby," I said.

It didn't sound enough. But I couldn't put all I felt into words.

John picked Louise as the baby's middle name, and left me to choose the first one. But Louise grew on us, so that's what she became. We asked Mr. and Mrs. Steptoe to choose a middle name for her instead.

Mr. Steptoe was a bit embarrassed. "We'll have to think about it," he said.

The next day, he told me that they both liked the name Joy. "That's what this baby's brought to you and John," he said.

So Louise Joy it became. The woman who registered her names got into such a state when she realised who the baby was that she kept making mistakes on the birth certificate. She tore up seven certificates before she managed to write a perfect one.

The day arrived when I had to take Louise home. Even before she was born, I had been dreading that. It was bad enough having that mob of reporters constantly outside the hospital, but now the thought of having to face them terrified me.

Being interviewed in hospital by the *Daily Mail* had been an ordeal. I'm just not the sort who enjoys all that fuss. I'd never been used to so many people being interested in me.

When the woman journalist from the *Mail* asked me if I'd seen my baby in the test tube, I nearly hit her over the head. I couldn't believe any one could be so ignorant when that part of it had only lasted two days.

A *Mail* photographer brought several expensive nightdresses for me to choose one to wear in the press photographs. The one I picked cost over a hundred pounds and I was allowed to keep it afterwards. But I didn't wear it for a long time. It just didn't seem right getting into bed in something that had cost so much.

John arrived early on the morning I was going home, to collect all the baby's things. There was a huge teddy bear, a new cot, loads of toys and clothes, and about four hundred letters and cards that had arrived from all over the world when Louise was born.

Mr. Steptoe came to my room and kissed me good-bye. Reporters had already surrounded the ambulance that was waiting outside to take Louise and me home.

"Make sure you look after that little baby," Mr. Steptoe said.

"I'll do the best I can," I replied.

Hospital officials surrounded me as a mob of re-porters rushed towards us as we emerged from a back door. A sister carried Louise, and I hobbled behind, since I still couldn't walk all that well.

Louise had her shawl over her face, and I bent my head as flashbulbs exploded around us and reporters shouted questions at me.

Faces of journalists were pressed at every window as

I sat in the ambulance. The driver hurriedly pulled down the blinds, but the worst was yet to come.

As we shot out of the hospital gates, I hung on tightly to Louise. Those newspaper men would stop at nothing to get at my baby.

I remembered the night at the hospital when a journalist started a bomb scare. Mrs. Steptoe had just arrived with a game of scrabble, and was about to teach me to play it, when the alarm bell rang. Mr. Steptoe came at once and took me out of my room in a wheel-chair.

It was alright for me. Everyone took such good care of me. But some of those women who had just had babies had to get up and walk on their own to other parts of the hospital, and a lot were in pain. I hung my head as I passed some of those mothers. The bomb scare had happened because I was in the hospital and I was ashamed to have caused so much trouble.

One woman even had her baby while it was going on. The press just didn't seem to care what they did to get a story.

The ambulance pulled up at a motorway cafe, as I was longing for a cup of tea. "She can't go in the cafe," said a *Daily Mail* reporter who was travelling with us. "Someone might recognise her."

How was I ever going to pop down to the local shops again?

It was pouring with rain as the reporter rushed me across the car park to a police hut. The ambulance driver looked after Louise while a policeman put the kettle on.

There was a two-way radio in the ambulance, and the driver was getting information about what was happening outside our house. The press had blocked the entrance with their cars, so it would have been impossible for us to pull up outside. After two months in hospital, I couldn't even get inside my own home.

The ambulance parked on a deserted speedway track on the outskirts of Bristol and, as the rain hammered on the roof, I gave Louise a feed. Luckily, she didn't know anything about it all. Once she'd had her bottle, she went fast off to sleep again.

After two hours parked at the speedway track, there was a message on the ambulance's radio that the police had moved the cars that were blocking the front of our house. The road was still jammed with television cameras and newspapermen. But they weren't going to leave until I got there, so we decided to make a dash for it.

A television microphone on a long black pole was poked into my face as soon as the ambulance door opened. The ambulance driver took Louise, hidden in her carry cot, and carried her over the heads of the crowd into our house.

That left me stuck in the back of the ambulance, struggling to get my cardigan on. The microphone was still being shoved in my face, and I couldn't get my arms into the cardigan. I got out of the ambulance with it half over my head.

Immediately, I was surrounded by the press. Newspapermen, cameras and microphones reached right up to our front door. There was no way I could get past all of them.

"John," I screamed. Suddenly I spotted him, clambering out of his car. Those reporters were too busy shouting questions to notice John fighting his way towards me.

A few people went flying, as he forced his way through. He grabbed me, pulled my cardigan off my head, and carried me through the mob to the house. Then he slammed the front door on the lot of them.

"Thank goodness I turned up when I did," he said. "At least I got you indoors with a bit of dignity left." I burst into tears.

I was home at last. But what a homecoming it was. Reporters pressed their faces at all of the downstairs windows. It was like being in a cage again.

The *Daily Mail* dragged me upstairs at once to be photographed in Louise's nursery.

Everything in the room was ready for Louise, except that John had forgotten to put back the net curtain I'd washed when I was last at home. As I glanced out of the bare window, telescopic cameras were trained on us from the roofs opposite, where Press photographers had clambered to get a better view.

"I'm now standing outside 4, Hassell Drive." Someone outside the kitchen window was speaking into a microphone. "It's a little council house that looks as if it hasn't had a coat of paint for years."

"What a tatty place," another reporter remarked, as those pressmen trampled over our garden.

"Go out and belt them," I told John. I'd hardly stopped crying since I'd been indoors.

"That's just what they're waiting for," John said. "We must ignore it. They'll go away soon."

It didn't seem as if they ever would.

But they all did clear off when it got dark. At last, the house felt normal again. But it wouldn't last. When morning came, all those journalists would be back.

A brand new pram stood in the hall, but it didn't seem worth having now. I couldn't imagine ever being able to take Louise outside the front door.

I was so afraid that first night that I wouldn't wake up when Louise cried. I needn't have worried though. That baby of ours had the loudest yell in the hospital, and when she started that night, I shot out of bed.

179

If the neighbours heard, they might let the newspapers know. I could imagine the headlines: "Test Tube Baby Screams All Night."

Having a miracle was a lot to live up to. It felt as if the whole world expected me to be a perfect mother.

CHAPTER SEVENTEEN

John sums up.

W HEN LOUISE FIRST came home, I was pushed right into the background by Les. I had expected that but, when it happened, it really hurt a lot.

I just wanted to be part of bringing the baby up. But, having given Les a child, it was as if I didn't matter any more.

The trouble was that I hadn't got any confidence in bathing the baby or changing her nappy, though I'd done all that for Sharon and Beverley when Margaret had walked out on me.

But all that fuss about Louise being a miracle had made me ham-fisted. If I'd dropped the baby, what a field day those reporters waiting outside would have had.

"Someone's got to be first, but why us?" I asked myself. "Why were Les and me chosen to have this baby?"

I had never had much in my life. I wasn't all that intelligent. We can only do the best we can for Louise.

Journalists knocked on the door all day, so I hired

Geoff, the security guard who had been outside Les' room in the hospital, to keep them away.

He was tactful, even when those pressmen put their feet in our door to stop him closing it. If it had been me, I would have slammed it with their feet still there.

Geoff was useful in all sorts of ways. He even hung the nappies on the line, since Les was still afraid to go outside.

Two weeks after Les and the baby came home, the reporters left us alone. So I went back to work.

"What's a wealthy bloke like you still driving a lorry for?" There were lots of snide remarks to put up with when I started my job again.

That money from the *Daily Mail* had turned out to be a nuisance as much as anything else. It had already caused trouble in the family.

A few of our neighbours had made money by selling pictures of Les and me to the press and by renting their roofs and gardens for the journalists to get a better view of our house. I couldn't blame them too much for that. But when some of our relations sold stories about us too, I just didn't know whom we could trust any more.

Les' brother Dave apologised for talking to the *Sunday People* and even wanted to send back a cheque from them.

"Don't be bloody daft," I said. At least Dave had been straight with us. There were other members of the family who had new bathroom suites and settees from jumping on the publicity bandwagon. But they wouldn't admit that they'd made money out of us.

Les hadn't been out of hospital long before we weren't on speaking terms with half the family. There was so much jealousy because they thought I was rolling in money. Yet, since we've had the *Daily Mail* cheque, I've hardly seen any of it. The money is out of my hands, being invested, so we've just enough to bring Louise up.

There's not a lot I'd want to buy myself, though I wouldn't mind owning my own lorry so I could be my own boss. There's a three-bedroomed house in Bristol that we'd like to buy as well, as the garden is perfect for Louise. There's even a sandpit and a swing, and, since it's secluded with lots of trees and shrubs, no one could spy on her.

Talk about money still goes straight over my head. All I know is that Les and I still seem as hard up as we've always been. The other Sunday I had £3 left in my pocket to last until pay day in four days' time.

Lately I've even had to start working at weekends, which was the one thing I thought I'd never have to do again after getting all that money from the *Mail*.

Louise will be a rich girl when she grows up. There's a trust fund being set up for her and Sharon, which will make Louise worth about a hundred thousand pounds by the time she's twenty-one. That's a lot more money than her Dad's ever likely to have. She'll have to grow up a sensible girl to cope with it.

If she's like Sharon, she could do a lot worse. We've never had any real worries over her. Sharon's courting now, but she's always in by eleven o'clock. She's never been one to gad about the streets late at night, like Les and I once did.

When Les went out to work, Sharon always had tea ready when we got in, and on weekends she'd clean the house from top to bottom. She's been as good as gold.

She idolises Louise, though she'll never be photographed with her by the press. What Sharon resents is all the fuss made over the baby's birth.

It must be hard for her to realise that she's always been just as special as Louise to us. Our feelings for Sharon were just as strong when Les and I got her out of the children's home as when Louise was born.

The trouble is that, having waited so long for Louise to turn up, I'm daft about her. Every father idolises his daughter, but I dote too much on mine.

After not even getting a look-in when she first came home, once I got confident with her, I couldn't leave her alone. I had to push the pram or carry her when we went out, and at home I wanted to do everything for her.

Now I force myself to let Louise cry, instead of grabbing her at the slightest opportunity. She's spoilt enough already, because everyone who meets her wants to pick her up and cuddle her.

"We mustn't over-protect her," I told Les. "If she bumps herself, we've got to grin and bear it. She's got to be treated like a normal child."

Directly after I had said that, Louise nearly fell off the bed. Les caught her by the pants just in time.

Every child's a miracle to its parents, and that's what we have to remember for Louise's sake.

She'll have an ordinary, state school education, unless she's clever, and then I'll use every penny I've got to do the best for her. I'd like her to go to university, as it was a chance that I never had.

But I won't push her into anything. All that really matters is that we've got her. I couldn't be without Louise now.

She's made me feel closer to Les as well. I don't have to bury my head in the pillow now when I tell the missus I love her, though Les still bites my head off if I say the wrong thing.

Les won't ever change, and neither will I. If we did, we would say goodbye to each other. It's our happiness and our sorrows that have made our marriage what it is.

And I'd live through every moment again, so long as it was with Les.

CHAPTER EIGHTEEN

And Lesley has the last word.

IT TOOK A MONTH after coming out of hospital for me to set foot outside that front door. Then I only went for Louise's sake. What worried me most was that she wasn't getting any fresh air.

The lady in the cake shop peered inside the pram. "Did you carry her in the same way as everyone else?" she asked. It was as if she expected a baby nine-inches long and one-inch wide. She'd imagined Louise had spent nine months, not two days, growing in a test tube.

People stared as we walked round the shops. Everyone who stopped me wanted to look in the pram. When they saw a normal child inside, they seemed surprised. It was as if they had expected a freak.

In the newsagents, a man pointed me out to another bloke. "You know who that is?" I heard him say.

"She's done alright for herself. She's well off through having that baby."

It hadn't occurred to me that anyone would think the reason we'd had Louise had been to make a lot of money.

When John had told me about how much we would get for our story from the *Daily Mail*, I didn't want to think about it. I had enough on my mind waiting for the baby to be born, and I'd never been all that interested in money.

But now that we had Louise, it was a different matter. I was glad we had enough to bring her up properly.

There was never any question of leaving Sharon out. She shares everything, because she's still just as much my child as she was from that day we took her out of the children's home.

Someone asked recently how my daughter was getting along. "Which one?" I asked. However special Louise's birth was, it hasn't made any difference. Sharon and Louise are both my daughters now.

I have got a lot closer to my own mother, too, since Louise has been born. She's always asking to look after the baby. She adores her.

"If I died, you wouldn't have Louise adopted?" I asked John. It was on my mind because he'd had his daughter Beverley adopted, and I couldn't bear the thought of Louise being brought up in a stranger's home.

"Circumstances were different then," he told me. "I just couldn't manage to bring up two children on my own."

I thought how Mum had never seemed to want Dave and me when we were young. Circumstances had been different for her as well.

Gran thought Louise was marvellous. John stood the carry cot on the backroom table, and she couldn't resist getting up every few minutes to have a peep at her.

"You've got everything you've ever wanted now," Gran told me.

Gran died last Christmas. John went round on

Boxing Day to pick her up so she could spend the day with us. It was too late to do anything. She must have died in her sleep during the night.

Gran was a mother to me. I don't know how I'd have got over it if I didn't have Louise.

But John would have still been around. Whatever he says, I still believe we'd have stuck together if Louise hadn't been born.

After all the years together, we're part of each other, just as now Louise is part of us both. I don't think he needs me to tell him that I love him. He knows that I do.

I've still had to tell him, though, to mind his own business when he kept advising me about how I should be looking after Louise.

But it's his business really. He's her father and he thinks the world of her too. So he's got every right to have his say.

"There's no such person as the perfect mother," the health visitor told me when I got Louise home. It really shocked me once when I shouted at the baby because she kept crying.

It wasn't a question of not loving her. It just seemed as if I didn't deserve her if I behaved like that.

There were so many childless women who would have made better mothers, if they'd been given the same chance.

"You just do the best you can," the health visitor told me. And that's what I try to do. But I've still got the feeling inside that I ought to be perfect, though I never will be.

Louise is special because she would never have been born at all in the normal way. It was a miracle that I was chosen to have her.

When Louise knows about her birth, I want her to feel proud as well.

Whatever happens in her life, I'll always believe that Louise was truly meant to be.